Digital Innovations and the Production of Local Content in Community Radio

This book offers an in-depth analysis of how local community radio practitioners have embraced the digital revolution.

Digital Innovations and the Production of Local Content in Community Radio contextualizes the UK model of community radio, before focussing on specific case studies to examine how the use of digital technologies has affected local radio production practices. The book offers an overview of the new technologies, media forms, and platforms in radio production, shedding light on how digitalization is impacting the routines and experiences of a predominantly volunteer-based workforce. The author presents the argument that despite the benefits of digital media, traditional aspects of programme production continue to be of vital importance to the interpersonal relationships and values of community radio.

This book will appeal to academics and researchers in the areas of communication, culture, journalism studies, media, and creative industries.

Josephine F. Coleman is Lecturer in Media and Public Relations at Brunel University London. Her first degree was in Geography from Cambridge. She has an MA in the History of Film and Visual Media and a PhD on community radio production practices from Birkbeck, University of London. She worked as promotions and PR Executive for an independent local radio network before joining Jazz FM in London. She later became a BBC local radio news journalist and presenter, having trained in community media both in the UK and in the USA. Josephine is also communications officer and former chair of the UK MeCCSA Radio Studies Network.

Disruptions: Studies in Digital Journalism

Series editor: Bob Franklin

Disruptions refers to the radical changes provoked by the affordances of digital technologies that occur at a pace and on a scale that disrupts settled understandings and traditional ways of creating value, interacting and communicating both socially and professionally. The consequences for digital journalism involve far reaching changes to business models, professional practices, roles, ethics, products and even challenges to the accepted definitions and understandings of journalism. For Digital Journalism Studies, the field of academic inquiry which explores and examines digital journalism, disruption results in paradigmatic and tectonic shifts in scholarly concerns. It prompts reconsideration of research methods, theoretical analyses and responses (oppositional and consensual) to such changes, which have been described as being akin to 'a moment of mind-blowing uncertainty'.

Routledge's new book series, *Disruptions: Studies in Digital Journalism*, seeks to capture, examine and analyse these moments of exciting and explosive professional and scholarly innovation which characterize developments in the day-to-day practice of journalism in an age of digital media, and which are articulated in the newly emerging academic discipline of Digital Journalism Studies.

What is Digital Journalism Studies?
Steen Steensen and Oscar Westlund

Changing News Use
Irene Costera Meijer and Tim Groot Kormelink

Crowdfunding and Crowdsourcing in Journalism
Andrea Hunter

Digital Innovations and the Production of Local Content in Community Radio
Josephine F. Coleman

For more information, please visit: www.routledge.com/Disruptions/book-series/DISRUPTDIGJOUR

Digital Innovations and the Production of Local Content in Community Radio

Changing Practices in the UK

Josephine F. Coleman

Routledge
Taylor & Francis Group

LONDON AND NEW YORK

First published 2021
by Routledge
2 Park Square, Milton Park, Abingdon, Oxon OX14 4RN

and by Routledge
605 Third Avenue, New York, NY 10017

Routledge is an imprint of the Taylor & Francis Group, an informa business

British Library Cataloguing-in-Publication Data
A catalogue record for this book is available from the British Library

Library of Congress Cataloging-in-Publication Data
Names: Coleman, Josephine F, author.
Title: Digital innovations and the production of local content in community radio : changing practices in the UK / Josephine F. Coleman.
Description: London ; New York : Routledge, 2021. | Includes bibliographical references and index. | Summary: "This book offers an in-depth analysis of how local community radio practitioners have embraced the digital revolution. Digital Innovations and the Production of Local Content in Community Radio contextualizes the UK model of community radio, before focusing on specific case studies to examine how the use of digital technologies has affected local radio production practices. The book offers an overview of the new technologies, media forms, and platforms in radio production, shedding light on how digitalisation is impacting the routines and experiences of a predominantly volunteer-based workforce. The author presents the argument that despite the benefits of digital media, traditional aspects of programme production continue to be of vital importance to the interpersonal relationships and values of community radio. This book will appeal to academics and researchers in the areas of communication, culture, journalism studies, media, and creative industries"-- Provided by publisher.
Identifiers: LCCN 2020049723 | ISBN 9780367507022 (hardback) | ISBN 9781003050865 (ebook)
Subjects: LCSH: Community radio--Great Britain--Case studies. | Community radio--Technological innovations.
Classification: LCC HE8697.95.G74 C65 2021 | DDC 384.5406/50941--dc23
LC record available at https://lccn.loc.gov/2020049723

ISBN 13: 978-0-367-50702-2 (hbk)
ISBN 13: 978-0-367-50700-8 (pbk)

Typeset in Times New Roman
by MPS Limited, Dehradun

To my parents, Susan and Mike, and to Tim, George, Olly and Ed.

Thank you for always being there.

Contents

1 Radio – a social technology   1
Introduction 1
Understanding radio as a social medium 4
Digital technologies and the meaning of radio 6
Community radio and its audiences 9
Conclusion 12

2 Framing community radio research   16
Introduction 16
Community radio in context – the global scene 17
   Where there's a will, there's a way 19
The evolution of non-mainstream radio in the UK 22
   Regulating the great British airwaves 22
   Pirate undercurrents 25
   Licensing community radio in the UK 27
   Funding and sustaining the sector 29
   Filling the local news gap 31
Researching local community radio stations 32
   The theory behind my methodological approach 33
   Studying radio production practices 35
   Creative practice-as-research 37
   Snapshot visits and participant observation 37
   Online (socially distanced) inquiry 38
Conclusion 39

3   Sites and sounds of community radio   44

Introduction 44
Home-produced local content for a hubless virtual
   radio station 44
   Scheduling issues 48
Producing content and building community at
   local stations 49
   103 The Eye – station base and family home 50
   Vibe 107.6 FM – high-tech studio and training
   centre 52
   Somer Valley 97.5 FM – community hub for
   educational training 55
   Radio LaB 97.1 FM – campus-based community
   station 58
   Radio Verulam 92.6 FM – local station and
   online hub 62
      Coverage of local current affairs 63
      Pre-recording content 65
      Voice-tracking 67
      Live shows 68
      Reporting and outside broadcasts 70
      Teamwork and training 72
      Lockdown response 73
Conclusion 74

4   Practitioners and content production   76

Introduction 76
The radio station as a place for community 77
The online spaces of community radio 79
Digital technologies and producing radio content 81
   Providing local coverage 83
      Sourcing 85
      Sifting 86
      Serving 87
      Saving 87
      Storing 87
      Shaping 88
      Sharing 88

Screening 89
Surveying 89
Diversity in community radio 89
The impact of COVID-19 on the production of local
content 93
Management approaches 94
Programme schedules 96
Community action stations 98
Conclusion 100

5 **Keeping radio local in the digital age**   104
Introduction 104
Reflections on "progress" and change 105
The enduring value of local radio 107
The business of community radio 109
Recommendations for future research and practice 112

Appendix: Table of community radio stations
researched for this study   116
Index   118

1 Radio – a social technology

Introduction

The aim of this book is to explore how digital innovations, tools and technologies have helped to shape contemporary radio production practices. The case studies employed here to generate evidence are illustrative of the UK community radio sector which, after decades of campaigning, was eventually legitimated in the early years of the 21st century. Perspectives on UK community media, however, are not featured so much in published research as those focussed on practice in other parts of the world; this book goes some way to redress that shortcoming. I suggest moreover, that the site-specific, practice-focussed framing of this study provides in-depth analysis of another under-explored but crucial aspect of media studies: the experiences of unpaid radio practitioners in the production of local(ized) and special interest content. Reflection on these matters yields important ethical insights which are of considerable value to media studies more generally.

To clarify, this book does not offer a technical account of the engineering and information technology (IT) aspects of the cable, wireless, broadcast or streamed transmission of radio signals. Rather, it explores how the practice of creating radio station output has been impacted by digital technologies and how the internet, as well as interactive social media platforms, have altered practitioners' routines, adding or detracting from the social and sociable experiences of the practice. In addition, the research methods informing the research reported in this book, demonstrate that digital technologies have improved and enriched how radio can be studied.

The original rationale for focussing on non-mainstream radio in this inquiry was that against the backdrop of the shifting broadcast media landscape, positioned between large corporate branded networks and a growing multitude of independent webcasters and podcasters, community radio seemed to have reached a turning point. Was this licensed, not-for-profit community sector the answer to enabling the provision of a dependable and genuinely local broadcasting service? And if so, could this be achieved and afforded by the licensed operators without compromising the utopian notion that community radio should be done for, with and by members of the targeted publics? Digital innovations had unleashed cheaper, easier ways of making audio content but what impact did this have on unpaid (non-professional or amateur) practitioner experiences in the community sector and on their relationships with their local (or locally-invested) listeners? How did different equipment and skill requirements change how radio stations were structured and how the working arrangements for their practitioners were organized? What did the term "radio station" mean anyway, when across the industry, traditional functions like engineering, music acquisition, publicity, sales, management, news reporting and presenting were less and less fixed to a single physical place? Most local community radio bases, or hubs, are modestly sized and cannot easily accommodate large groups. Stations remain accessible to their publics but nowadays, listeners can "visit" a website or Facebook page to interact with the staff, rather than go to the building itself. Indeed, in some cases, thanks to advances in electronic media, it is not uncommon for entire programmes to be produced off-site, in remote studios or spare bedrooms and uploaded to station servers for later broadcast.

COVID-19, however, has been an unexpected crisis, demanding agility and innovation in both societal and individual responses to the imposed conditions of social distancing and lockdown. In all walks of life, everyday practices changed to accommodate the very different structural arrangements within which we were all expected to function. The use of digital media technologies, devices, platforms and apps soared in both the public sphere – governmental, business and third sector – and in private, domestic domains. This "turn to the virtual" threw into sharp relief how digital technologies were being harnessed by community radio station teams in pursuit of their key commitments through local broadcasting for social gain. My interdisciplinary research was conducted before and during the pandemic and comprised a combination of desk research, a practice-as-research project, participant observation and snapshot station visits, interviews and an online questionnaire. The purpose was to explore the use of digital technologies in particular local community radio stations and later to test the assumption that introducing wholescale reliance on them automatically empowers all practitioners.

In this first chapter, I introduce the subject matter by discussing the ways in which theorists understand key concepts relating to and associated with radio: mass communication and broadcasting; audio content and related outputs; and social discourse. The overview of academic discourse about radio continues as I explore what has been written about the medium's relationship with technology, especially in the light of more recent digital innovations. I then consider in more depth the association of radio broadcasting with notions of place, community-building and belonging. In Chapter Two, I present an overview of community radio and how the seeds of what became a global movement for popular access to the airwaves were eventually allowed to germinate in the UK when the sector was established to satisfy the demand for local, niche interest radio. I then outline briefly how my research was framed and conducted.

Chapter Three is replete with descriptions and anecdotes from the case studies and research which convey how locally relevant features and programme content are produced by the predominantly volunteer producers and presenters in UK community radio stations. The focus is on how I perceived digital devices and software being routinely incorporated into performances of the practice, which were shaped by and shaped the material and organizational arrangements in the sampled station settings. Here, I begin to reveal how COVID-19 influenced that usage and differentially impacted the practitioner experience. In Chapter Four, I analyse my fieldwork findings and contextualize them against a variety of indicators about the wider sector gleaned from the online questionnaire conducted as the crisis unfolded. I discuss contemporary production environments, comparing normal with crisis conditions, and ponder the interwoven connections and interrelations with local communities that practitioners navigated in their quest to produce locally sourced and resonant content. I highlight how softer journalistic approaches and the nurturing of social networks facilitated their practice.

In the concluding Chapter Five, I reflect on how radio broadcasting and production practices have changed in relation to the provision of local content for non-mainstream community stations. The enduring value of local media and the increasing interest in living and consuming locally contribute to my arguments for more attention to be paid to how local community radio can be provided for in the future to sustain the sector. I urge that digital technologies be applied, and radio stations set up and resourced, in ways which benefit and enable everyone who is entitled to be a part of a community radio station to join in and have their voice aired.

Understanding radio as a social medium

Radio broadcasting technology was developed around the turn of the 20th century from earlier experiments in wireless telegraphy. The achievement is ascribed to Guglielmo Marconi whose projects were initially for military clients before turning to the medium's potential for domestic usage. Radio radically changed the communication of messages because the sound of actual voices could be transmitted in real time over distance, eliminating the barriers of time and space. In his book *Understanding media: the extensions of man* (1964), Canadian theorist Marshall McLuhan describes the electronic medium as one of the "new media and technologies by which we amplify and extend ourselves" (McLuhan, 1964, p. 64). His famous phrase coined at the time, "global village", and his concern over whether this heightened sense of proximity to other people(s) would be a force for good, rings true in today's media-saturated, internet-connected world.

In the 1930s, artists and writers were intrigued by the paradox of the medium's affective immateriality over time and space and urged that the medium's power of expression be used for positive purposes. They believed in radio's utopian potential. Rudolf Arnheim, convinced that radio programmes should address audiences' common needs, writes that: "Wireless without prejudice serves everything that implies dissemination and community of feeling and works against separateness and isolation" (Arnheim, 1936, p. 252). In *The stuff of radio* (1934), BBC producer Lance Sieveking describes radio as a machine: one which could achieve "sudden mental contact" between listener and broadcaster (Sieveking, 1934, pp. 111–112, 101). Berthold Brecht, best known for his stage plays, was a radio presenter and experimented in radio theatre. He wrote a lecture about the potential of radio for connecting people and encouraging their participation in society and politics (Brecht, 1932).

Those in political circles, however, feared the use of radio for propaganda and indeed the medium had been used tactically during the Second World War. Sociologists in the USA investigated how radio as a form of mass media could influence social change, but found that its power lay more in persuasion than propaganda (Lazarsfeld and Merton, [1948] 1975, pp. 497–501). Research indicated that members of the public needed to be predisposed to engaging with a particular message. Changing basic attitudes only happened when "in conjunction with face-to-face contacts" (ibid., p. 512).

As academic interest shifted in the 1960s towards the critical, visual text-based study of films and television programmes, the development of radio studies as a discipline stalled (Hilmes and Loviglio, 2002). This has been explained by the medium's evanescence, and the complications of capturing specific radio programmes to store and study as texts in classroom settings (Starkey and Crisell, 2009, p. 1). Research on the medium was occasionally published by sociologists and practitioners, exploring the act and effectiveness of radio presenting. Erving Goffman for instance listened intently to live radio, tape recordings and vinyl records for his chapter "Radio talk" in *Forms of talk* (Goffman, 1981, p. 197). This study inspired further radio-focussed work such as Paddy Scannell and Graham Brand's "Talk, identity and performance" in which they describe how a "discursive space" is created in radio programmes: a sense of a shared virtual space conveying a spirit of sociability (Scannell, 1991, p. 223). Scannell highlights the importance of personability conveyed by the on-air voices because listeners "expected to be spoken to in a familiar, friendly and informal manner as if they were equals on the same footing as the speaker" (ibid., p. 3).

Scannell's further work on phenomenological aspects of broadcasting marked a turn towards focussing on the emotional and affective impacts experienced by audiences (Scannell 1996), which would later be developed by media theorist Shaun Moores. Scannell acknowledges the recursive nature of social life, how broadcasting schedules are planned around it to reproduce patterns and routines, reinforcing a framework of "dailiness" and "eventfulness" (Scannell, 1996 in Moores, 2005, p. 9). This continuity in daily life that people can identify with is reassuring and Moores cites eminent sociologist Anthony Giddens' concept of "ontological security"; we find comfort in the knowledge that life goes on, that there is a constancy in our surroundings (Moores, 2005, p. 11). Listeners develop their own rituals of listening and use radio to mark their time. In a subsequent book, Moores describes how the constant rounds of discursive exchanges, of episodic series and regular programme slots fixed into the broadcast schedules become mediated "places" that audiences tune in to regularly and come to take for granted (Moores, 2012, p. 32). He argues that media-related interactions and experiences happen in these virtual places but are always rooted in physical localities, creating a spatial pluralization (Moores, 2012, p. 16). Wherever a listener is located, they can feel as if they are experiencing other actual localities being invoked on-air as well as the imagined radio studio.

This advanced theorization of radio became more prevalent as digital technologies became more readily available. Enhanced research methods meant that radio production methods and outputs could be studied more easily, and in more depth, to investigate those qualities such as liveness, intimacy and affective power. Scholars have discussed the "arbitrariness" and "secondariness" of this audio-only medium (Crisell, 1986, p. 213). Yet at the same time, radio listening is recognized as a vital daily ritual, even an emotional crutch, as "a domestic accompaniment ... which ... aids mood creation and maintenance" (Tacchi, 2009, p. 174). Notwithstanding the technological basis of the medium and how it seemed to be evolving so rapidly, theorists continued to describe radio as a social medium, to account for the human elements involved in communication: with a sometimes controversial role to play in the public sphere (Hilmes, 1997). The production and dissemination of meaningful content through speech and combinations of sounds and music are cultural activities and as such carry implications for the shaping of social discourse.

Towards the end of the 20th century, radio studies emerged as a separate discipline thanks to the collective effort of academics around the world sharing an intellectual passion for the field (Lewis 1998, 2000). Initiatives included the launch of the *Journal of Radio & Audio Media* and *The Radio Journal* as well as The Radio Studies Network in 1998. At an international conference held in Cardiff University, Wales, in 1999, *Radio, democracy and development*, the central theme was "radiocracy", a term conceived at a Commonwealth Press Union conference in Cape Town three years previously, which reflected the widely held and deep-seated belief in the democratizing potential of the medium. In 2009, an impressive three-volume edited collection of a century's worth of published work on radio was curated, *Radio: critical concepts in media and cultural studies* (Crisell, 2009), including articles and extracts from: Brecht's utopian assertion of the two-way communicative benefits of wireless radio broadcasting (Brecht, 1932); Donald McWhinnie's chapter on "The nature of the medium: the experience" from *The art of radio* (McWhinnie, 1959); Jo Tacchi's call for better theorizing of radio since the advent of digital "radiogenic" technologies (Tacchi, 2000); and Richard Berry's discussion of the disruptive potential of podcasting (Berry, 2006).

Digital technologies and the meaning of radio

In the book *International Radio Journalism*, Tim Crook acknowledges this "Radio Renaissance" and celebrates the "medium that has never lost its importance and value to human society" (Crook, 1997, p. 4). Crook's guide for students provides historical context to the craft, as he recalls the analogue mixing process, working with reel-to-reel tape, editing with chinagraph pencils and razor blades, and using CD-ROMs (read-only compact discs) for data retrieval. He admits that had he written the book when originally commissioned in the 1980s, it would have been out of date within two years due to the "new technological revolution which has radically changed the efficiency and way that radio journalists can operate" (ibid.). Theorists described the internet as a "Wild West" of opportunities. The ability to surf for up-to-date information on a global scale impacted on the ability of media producers to source and check programme content. With the introduction of webcasting from 1995, radio programmes could be streamed online which also facilitated academic research. Material being accessible from further afield and available for longer periods of time provided new ways of monitoring and assessing broadcast and other outputs as well as audience engagement, thus enabling more widely informed radio inquiries. Researchers found that the internet offered broadcasters "with vision and foresight" opportunities "to supplement their stations without supplanting them ... a way of strengthening brand loyalty while offering services not easily provided through broadcasting" (Lind and Medoff, 1999, p. 220). Websites were not only informational they were promotional: "another tool in the manager's marketing arsenal to support his/her station image and awareness" (Hamula and Williams, 2003, p. 263).

No wonder theorists had begun to question what business radio was in, as Berry points out in his chapter heralding a hybrid future of "visually-driven or socially-interactive content" (Berry, 2014, p. 12). With convergence occurring in organizational and operational spheres resulting in bi-media and multimedia outputs, one might have wondered whether the term "radio" was still appropriate. Innovations such as streaming, remediation of broadcast audio, podcasting and visualization have disrupted contemporary understandings of what radio content can be: what forms it can take and what platforms it can be consumed on (Freire, 2008; Berry, 2016). Michele Hilmes explains: "Today radio is a screen medium: we access it through screens both mobile and static, using tactile visual and textual interfaces ... Radio crosses platforms" (Hilmes and Loviglio, 2013, p. 44). Online interactivity has broadened the ways the public engage. Text messaging and email and before that by letter, these methods continue, but as Tiziano Bonini describes: "the information, filtered and re-elaborated, is then transformed in new content ready to enter the radio flow" (Bonini, 2014). Social media, such as Facebook and Twitter, are now extensively incorporated into radio programming (Bonini et al., 2014). Thus, though radio stations are increasingly in the business of creating and distributing multimedia content, they continue to schedule presenter-led audio programmes and interact with listeners.

The blurring of boundaries in the way radio stations produce and share entertainment and information has served to heighten academic interest in the field. Shifts in the media technology landscape have prompted a sonic turn in cultural studies (Lacey, 2013, p. 4), and have inspired media historians to explore histories of listening and the notion of "having a voice". Kate Lacey recounts how acts of listening have evolved and considers that in relation to the contemporary public sphere, political agency implies that one must not only find a voice, but find people who will listen (ibid., p. viii). David Hendy has described hopes that the introduction of digital technologies would increase democratic participation through enabling alternative voices to access the airwaves as "microbroadcasters", when "entry costs and technical skills" became cheap enough to set up stations online (Hendy, 2000, pp. 218–219). Writing at the turn of the 21st century, just before the community radio sector was launched in the UK, Hendy describes in political economy terms how the digitalization of radio impacts the industry in two ways: production and distribution (ibid., p. 213). In his article, he discusses the regulatory environment in the UK and the supposition that digital audio broadcast (DAB) frequencies would open up more space on the electromagnetic spectrum, increasing the number of stations and therefore listener choice (ibid., p. 217). He predicted that listener adoption would be slow, that the economies of scale would disproportionately benefit larger organizations broadcasting the same content over more channels, potentially leading to more company takeovers (ibid., p. 224).

Other early 21st century commentators have described the new wave of Web 2.0 interactivity as heralding an era of co-creation, in which consumers of the media are said to have become more involved in its production. Digital technologies have enabled the merging or convergence of producers and consumers (Jenkins, 2006). The "produser" not only consumes or uses content for entertainment and information purposes on media platforms and devices but can source, shape and share her own content across media channels. As a type of fandom, such produsage has taken off over the internet as circulating memes, constructed of images or video clips and a few words of ironic text. As a mode of commentary on current affairs, people create posts that go viral on social media channels celebrating, critiquing or attacking the ideas and actions of others. Arguably, such media content represents grassroots audience empowerment and freedom of expression enabled by digital technology. Anthropologist, Elizabeth Bird, cites Axel

Bruns' hope that produsage would grow from being the practice of a small minority to become the norm; this "could rekindle a desire on their part to once again become active produsers of democracy, rather than mere passive audiences" (Bruns, 2006, p. 9 in Bird, 2011, p. 511). Content creation by audiences is not directly of interest to this book, but how presenters and producers engage with them in the search for content is. It is beyond the current scope to discuss suggestions that audiences are exploited through their online interactions: the spectre of Web 3.0 relating to the use of algorithms whereby our every click or swipe when consuming and enjoying media is translated into commercially valuable marketing intelligence. How audiences physically consume radio is also beyond my scope, though I take on board that "commodification of haptically mediated listening" is happening and have some sympathy with idealistic notions of freeing data "from the aspirations of the market, and instead using them to foster digital commons" (Gazi and Bonini, 2018, p. 122). My aim instead is to focus on practitioners and the experience of being a broadcaster. To further tighten the focus, my research concentrates on what could be regarded as related to grassroots production but is the sector that has been institutionalized within the licensing framework of broadcasting in the UK as community radio.

Community radio and its audiences

Understanding how digital technologies enable and enhance community radio within the wider context of the broadcasting industry is important because it takes us back to the fundamental belief in radio as a potential means for expression, enabling everyone to have a voice and to have their voice heard. The social aspects of radio, which are manifest in the content derived from and generating engagement and interaction, are particularly valued in community broadcasting. We are reminded of the original high hopes for the medium: that everyone should have access to the airwaves to express themselves, and for their own life stories and interests to be represented. For scholars of radio, there is a firmly held conviction that radio and community do not simply coincide, they coexist in those virtual spaces that media create. In the introduction of *Radio content in the digital age* (2011), published following a conference in 2009 held by the Radio Research Section of the European Communication Research and Education Association (ECREA), the editors state: "community radio groups are already exploiting the opportunities of participation in the digitization of radio" (Gazi et al., 2011, p. 13).

Despite this show of enthusiasm, there has been a tendency in media and communication studies to overlook phenomena which are local in scale and scope, so it follows that there exist "those who might be tempted to dismiss community media as concerned with local trivia" (Atton, 2015, p. 7). As I proceed with the framing for my research to focus on localized case studies, it will become clear that I concur with Chris Atton's argument that research on local community media has wider significance for studies of media power since "amateur media practices may be embedded in everyday life practices" (ibid.). I too, see these arrays of practice as not only located in but inseparable from, "broader political, economic, social and cultural contexts" (ibid.). Mundane as the realm of "everyday cultural production" in community radio contexts may first appear, and even if their activities are not overtly political, the ways citizens harness the power of media to express themselves and improve their lot warrants our critical attention (Atton, 2002, p. 73). As Nick Couldry has remarked, "the ethical issues of the local – the spaces of family, friendship, institutions – are also entangled in, and transformed by, the flows of media on all scales" (Couldry, 2012, p. 28).

Defining community radio as a field of study is challenging due to the complexity of differing "felt needs" of the communities that are served (Howley, 2010, p. 2). Kevin Howley is referring to the global dimensions of community media here, and indeed British community radio has its unique characteristics, although there are also commonalities. I will discuss its history in the following chapter and demonstrate why, even in a national context, attention to specificity is required. There is also a conceptual complication with the very term "community". In her article, "The myth of community studies" (1969), Margaret Stacey questions whether the concept has any use as an abstraction in sociological analysis. She recommends we study "social relations in localities" to identify the organization, that is, the structure and process, of social systems through placing an emphasis on interrelations in time and space (Stacey, 1969, pp. 140–141). With this in mind and applying a practice-centric approach, I understand community in a geographical setting as sets of relations that people participate in locally. As I will explain later, these place-based social activities are sources of programme material. The interactions involved in these types of social and relational practices that materialize as institutions, clubs and membership societies can also happen online, where we find "people, technologies and other cultural artefacts ... co-producing new forms of residential sociality" (Postill, 2008, p. 426).

Understanding a station's audience as a community is also possible when we consider people in a spatial relationship with a particular locality taking on the position of listener from time to time. Through the act of listening, they play an active role in the "social sonic space" (Blaakilde, 2018, p. 294). Rarely though do we find a place saturated in a single cultural tradition, inhabited by people inspired by the same beliefs and driven by the same desires. The relative ease, frequency and extensiveness of mobility, whether physical or virtual, results in a host of different ways of experiencing the world and encountering other people within it (Urry, 2002, p. 263). Localities where we live are open to the world, so any community or neighbourhood will have "multiple identities" (Massey, 1994 in Moores, 2012, p. 77). Asking what local means in the context of a community radio station cannot simply be answered by referring to the transmission map and the radius of the signal. Listeners may travel into the area to work or study, and not necessarily reside within those boundaries. Identifying what content will be of interest and value to a local audience is a complex process. Everyone will have different experiences in everyday life and different expectations of what counts as local, but the aim still is to encourage engagement in building and nurturing meaningful community relations among users of those places in common (Lynne Anderson in Mair et al., 2012, pp. 258–259).

In practice, reflecting the local community back to itself is not so straightforward to achieve. For instance, finding an appropriate angle in a news story can be problematic in terms of achieving relevance and resonance across an entire audience when one takes into account the different interests according to any cultural differences, age, class or gender. What must also be taken into consideration is the permeability of locality, the global influences upon people's attitudes and sensibilities, which geographer Doreen Massey describes as "'outwardlookingness' ... a positivity and aliveness to the world beyond one's own turf" (Massey, 2005, p. 15 in Moores, 2012, p. 81). Media sociologist, Meryl Aldridge argues that "life is global; living is local" (Aldridge, 2007, p. 5); media's role is to facilitate debate and local input is imperative. She describes locality as "the arena for multiple forms of 'getting by' based on long-standing social networks ..." (ibid., p. 11). For community radio to be successful then, requires achieving "considerable diversity in their programme schedules and high levels of volunteer participation" (Browne, 2012, p. 166).

If media demonstrate "simple, local, community-connectedness" (Forde, 2011, p. 91), and persuade audiences to feel a part of things and have their say, by this logic, the volunteer practitioners recruited ought to be representative of all segments of the target audience to ensure everyone's views and values can be covered. This way, the on-air, online and off-air activities of community radio contribute towards the formation and maintenance of social ties linked to the locality. Station teams deliver their localized service by featuring local news, information and entertainment across a range of shows. This is achieved routinely through features ranging from local weather updates and traffic and travel, listing local events and campaigns, to interviewing people involved in local happenings, having local talent perform on-air and conducting live on-location reports or outside broadcasts. The volunteers dedicating a great part of their lives to performing this service are the practitioners at the heart of this book.

Conclusion

So far, I have discussed the sociable and discursive characteristics of radio broadcasting: station teams aim to involve audiences by the way music choices are made and communicated, and with other entertainments and information shared through engaging presenter chatter and conversations with studio or phone-in guests. Listening to the radio can affect the moods and emotions of audience members, sometimes content is experienced in ways that induce physical reactions. Producing and presenting shows, engaging in real or imagined dialogue through which relationships with listeners are formed, is also an affective experience. Doing radio has a physiological effect on the practitioners; they experience the "buzz". It is an intimate medium, it feels live and immediate, and is further enhanced by two-way interactive engagement online.

    Community media and local radio matter in the UK because of the retrenchment of mainstream media, which threatens to leave whole regions and groups of people underinformed about current affairs pertaining to local governance, and also potentially underequipped to react to any local ramifications of national and international events. This book explores how digital technologies have been central to the practice and experience of doing local community radio. It aims to highlight the important work of unpaid radio practitioners. The research has been gleaned largely from licensed community stations, but there is common ground with practitioners on local internet stations, podcasters, independent producers and hyperlocal media organizations. Chapter Two delves further into the framing of the research that informed this study. I provide some background to the international community radio scene, then discuss how the licensed community sector sits in the radio landscape in the UK, primarily as a group of broadcast providers of localized and special interest content.

References

Aldridge, M., 2007. *Understanding the Local Media*. McGraw-Hill/Open University Press, Maidenhead.

Arnheim, R., 1936. *Radio*. Faber & Faber, London.

Atton, C., 2002. *Alternative Media*. SAGE Publications, London.

Atton, C. (ed.), 2015. *The Routledge Companion to Alternative and Community Media*. Routledge, London and New York.

Berry, R., 2006. Will the iPod kill the radio star? Profiling podcasting as radio. *Convergence 12* (2), 143–162. 10.1177/1354856506066522.

Berry, R., 2014. The future of radio is the internet, not on the internet. In: Oliveira, M., Stachyra, G., Starkey, G. (eds.), *Radio: The Resilient Medium*. Papers from the Third Conference of the ECREA Radio Research Section. Centre for Research in Media and Cultural Studies, University of Sunderland, 3–16.

Berry, R., 2016. Podcasting: considering the evolution of the medium and its association with the word "radio". *Radio J. Int. Stud. Broadcast. Audio Media 14* (1), 7–22. 10.1386/rjao.14.1.7_1.

Bird, E.S., 2011. Are we all produsers now? *Cult. Stud. 25* (4–5), 502–516. 10.1080/09502386.2011.600532.

Blaakilde, A.L., 2018. The becoming of radio bodies. *Eur. J. Cult. Stud. 21* (3), 290–304. 10.1177/1367549417708437.

Bonini, T., *et al.*, 2014. Radio formats and social media use in Europe – 28 case studies of public service practice. *Radio J. Int. Stud. Broadcast. Audio Media 12* (1–2), 89–107. 10.1386/rjao.12.1-2.89_1.

Bonini, T., 2014. The new role of radio and its public in the age of social network sites, *First Monday. 19* (6). 10.5210/fm.v19i6.4311.

Brecht, B., 1932. Radio as a means of communication: a talk on the function of radio. *Screen 20* (3–4), 24–28. 10.1093/screen/20.3-4.24 Translated by S. Hood.

Browne, D.R., 2012. What is "community" in community radio? A consideration of the meaning, nature and importance of a concept. In: Gordon, J. (ed.), *Community Radio in the 21st Century*. Peter Lang, Bern, Switzerland, 153–173.

Couldry, N., 2012. *Media, Society, World: Social Theory and Digital Media Practice*. Polity Press, Cambridge.

Crisell, A., 1986. *Understanding Radio*. Methuen, London.

Crisell, A., 2009. *Radio. Critical Concepts in Media and Cultural Studies* (3 volumes). Routledge, London.

Crook, T., 1997. *International Radio Journalism – History, Theory & Practice*. Routledge, London; New York. http://research.gold.ac.uk/14104/ (accessed 06.11.18.).

Forde, S., 2011. *Challenging the News: The Journalism of Alternative and Community Media*. Palgrave Macmillan, Basingstoke, Hampshire; New York.

Freire, A.M., 2008. Remediating radio: audio streaming, music recommendation and the discourse of radioness. *Radio J. Int. Stud. Broadcast. Audio Media 5* (2), 97–112. 10.1386/rajo.5.2-3.97_1.

Gazi, A., Bonini, T., 2018. "Haptically Mediated" radio listening and its commodification: the remediation of radio through digital mobile devices, *J. Radio Audio Media 25* (1), 109–125. 10.1080/19376529.2017.1377203.

Gazi, A., Jedrzejewski, S., Starkey, G. (eds.), 2011. *Radio Content in the Digital Age: The Evolution of a Sound Medium*. Intellect, Bristol, UK; Chicago, USA.

Goffman, E., 1981. *Forms of Talk*. Blackwell, Oxford.

Hamula, S.R., Williams Jr., W., 2003. The internet as a small-market radio station promotional tool. *J. Radio Stud. 10* (2), 262–269. 10.1207/s15506843jrs1002_10.

Hendy, D., 2000. A political economy of radio in the digital age. *J. Radio Stud. 7* (1), 213–234. 10.1207/s15506843jrs0701_16.

Hilmes, M., 1997. *Radio Voices: American Broadcasting, 1922–1952*. University of Minnesota Press, Minneapolis; London.

Hilmes, M., Loviglio, J. (eds.), 2002. *Radio Reader: Essays in the Cultural History of Radio*. Routledge, London; New York.

Hilmes, M. and Loviglio, J. (eds.), 2013. *Radio's New Wave. Global Sound in the Digital Era*. Routledge, New York; London https://www.book2look.com/book/bn6w5MdYUk (accessed 28.10.18.).

Howley, K. (ed.), 2010. *Understanding Community Media*. SAGE Publications, London.

Jenkins, H., 2006. Introduction: worship at the altar of convergence, *Convergence Culture: Where Old and New Media Collide*. New York University Press, New York, 1–24.

Lacey, K., 2009. Ten years of radio studies: the very idea. *Radio J. Int. Stud. Broadcast. Audio Media 6* (1), 21–32. doi: 10.1386/rajo.6.1.21_4.

Lacey, K., 2013. *Listening Publics: The Politics and Experience of Listening in the Media Age*. Polity Press, Cambridge, UK; Malden, MA.

Lazarsfeld, P.F., Merton, R.K., 1975. Mass communication, popular taste and organized social action. In: Schramm, W. (ed.), *Mass Communication*. The University of Illinois Press, Urbana, 492–512.

Lewis, P.M., 1998. Radio theory and community radio, *Meeting 3: Theory and Methodology in Local Radio and Television Section. Local Radio and Television Section*. IAMCR, Glasgow.

Lewis, P.M., 2000. Private passion, public neglect: the cultural status of radio. *Int. J. Cult. Stud. 3* (2), 160–167.

Lind, R.A., Medoff, N.J., 1999. Radio stations and the world wide web. *J. Radio Stud. 6* (2), 203–221. 10.1080/19376529909391723.

Mair, J., Fowler, N., Reeves, I. (eds.), 2012. *What Do We Mean by Local? Grassroots Journalism – Its Death and Rebirth*. Abramis, Bury St Edmunds, UK.

McLuhan, M., 1964. *Understanding Media: The Extensions of Man*. Routledge & K. Paul, London.

McWhinnie, D., 1959. *The Art of Radio*. Faber & Faber, London.

Moores, S., 2005. *Media/Theory: Thinking About Media and Communications*. Routledge, London.

Moores, S., 2012. *Media, Place and Mobility.* Palgrave Macmillan, Basingstoke, UK.

Postill, J., 2008. Localising the internet beyond communities and networks. *N. Media Soc. 10* (3), 413–431.

Sieveking, L., 1934. *The Stuff of Radio.* Cassell, London.

Scannell, P. (ed.), 1991. *Broadcast Talk.* SAGE Publications, London, New Delhi.

Scannell, P., 1996. *Radio, Television, and Modern Life: a Phenomenological Approach.* Blackwell, Oxford.

Stacey, M., 1969. The myth of community studies. *Br. J. Sociol. 20* (2), 134–147.

Starkey, G., Crisell, A., 2009. *Radio Journalism.* SAGE Publications, London.

Tacchi, J., 2000. The need for radio theory in the digital age. *Int. J. Cult. Stud. 3* (2), 289–298.

Tacchi, J., 2009. Radio and affective rhythm in the everyday. *Radio J. Int. Stud. Broadcast. Audio Media 7* (2), 171–183.

Urry, J., 2002. Mobility and proximity. *Sociology 36* (2), 255–274.

Wright Mills, C., 1956. The mass society. In: *The Power Elite.* Oxford University Press, New York, pp. 298–324.

2 Framing community radio research

Introduction

Having established what meanings are understood and implied by the terms radio, audience and community, I now turn to the unique nature of community radio in the UK compared to other models around the world. Only a few academics continue researching this area, others are drawn into studying mainstream broadcasting or taking an international angle. There is a particular lack of scholarship about non-urban or suburban community radio stations in this relatively affluent and comparatively peaceful country. My site-specific case studies will help to rectify that but will also contribute new information and understandings to the global corpus. The core mission of the UK community sector is to provide social gain or benefit to the target communities and listening publics. The challenge is how to prove the social worth of these activities and convert the goodwill and achievements into vital resources to keep the stations afloat. This is often discussed at community radio networking events, on social media platforms and occasionally in the British press. The issue that is always on the agenda is what station managers and practitioners can or should be doing to raise the sector's public profile. Some research evidence is published and shared in academic circles supporting their case, but not as much as one might expect. To place UK licensed community radio in context, I first provide some background to the international scene and refer to examples of academic research and global variants of community radio: alternative non-mainstream, grassroots, activist. Then, I outline the development of the largely volunteer-run sector and how it has evolved into the country's provider of local coverage. I consider the issue of sustaining operations and how researching production practices within the sector can contribute useful knowledge to enhancing its offer and future opportunities. I explain the practice-centric framing used to identify the objects of my inquiry and to establish the fieldwork objectives. Using the example of my doctoral research, I discuss the concept of "social sites" of practice and the benefits of incorporating practice-as-research into the methodological mix. I discuss how digital technologies aided access to sources of information for desk research when exploring the practice of others and the importance of being mindful to reduce disruption when observing the routines of the participants in the field.

Community radio in context – the global scene

Academic literature reflects the reality that different radio broadcasting service models have been established around the world, depending on government involvement and ideologically driven intervention strategies. In her article, "History of struggle" (2017), Gretchen King acknowledges "the different origins of the practice and ... the common roots of community radio" (King, 2017, p. 30). She usefully charts four main periods in its development within a global context: the experimental decades 1900s–1940s; wildfire 1950s–1960s; solidarity 1970s–1980s; and resurgence from the 1990s onwards. Addressing claims that there persists a western-centric bias to community radio scholarship, King engages with the decolonizing debate. My interpretation of this situation is that there has been a preference in "First World" universities for conducting action research abroad pursuing communication for development aims, because these worthy projects can attract greater funding awards. However, I perceive plenty of research also being conducted and published by home-grown academics in developing countries and the Global South. In fact, I would argue that Western or UK-specific case studies are few and far between (see also Cammaerts, 2009).

I concur that there has been "scholarly neglect for the global story of community radio within media studies" (King, 2017, p. 21), although, the resurgence of radio studies around the turn of the 21st century heralded a refreshed worldwide community spirit and generated a good deal of research in the field. There are regular annual and biennial conferences attracting international radio and community media researchers, educators and scholars run by organizations such as the International Communication Association (ICA). Their 2018 conference in Prague opened with a plenary, "Communication and the Evolution of Voice", in which a panel including a representative from Radio Free Europe/Radio Liberty, discussed ways of studying and addressing issues concerning how citizens' voices were changing over time and space. There are ongoing efforts to maintain specialist sections and projects in other associations such: ECREA's Radio Research Section; the UK based scholarly body for Media, Communication and Cultural Studies Association's (MeCCSA) radio studies and local and community media networks; and the International Association for Media and Communications Research's (IAMCR) Community Communication and Alternative Media Section and the Music Audio Radio & Sound (MARS) working group.

The COVID-19 crisis in 2020 resulted in IAMCR's July conference proceedings shifting from the intended venue in Tampere, Finland to virtual platforms. The association's regional Media and Communication Research conference held in India the following month was delivered through webinars, too, using Facebook, YouTube and the now ubiquitous cloud-based video/chat software of Zoom Video Communications. These sessions were available to both members and non-members of IAMCR, demonstrating their intent to democratize access to new knowledge, notwithstanding the requirement to have a device and internet access in order to participate. Other organizations similarly held events online and by doing so were incentivized to build their social media networks in order to widen participation. Radio Days Africa for instance celebrated #TheNewNormal across Facebook, Instagram and Twitter with their educational conference for media and broadcast professionals and practitioners held during July. One of the 20 Zoom sessions was entitled, "Snakes and Ladders, the State of Community Radio in South Africa", in which a panel of experts discussed why community radio in South Africa is undervalued and underrated. The United Nations Educational, Scientific and Cultural Organization (UNESCO) Chair on Community Media organized an informative series of panels "Global Dialogues, Community Media in the Post-Pandemic World" that brought together practitioners and academics from around the world.

Digital technologies have increased international engagement and facilitated these improved communication networks for media researchers, practitioners and others in the business. Technological advances have also caused and at least correlate with a range of sociocultural, ethical, moral and political-economic issues with which academics are grappling. The discourse surrounding convergence and conglomeration in the media industries articulates concern over levels of public trust in media providers, the authenticity of output, fake news and so forth, generating a renewed interest in the utopian vision of media by and for the people. Academics the world over are forging improved links and connections with each other thanks to the internet and social media, responding to calls for conference presentations, journal papers and chapter proposals pivoting around a familiar shared dilemma: if knowledge and access to information is power, in whose hands does or should it lie?

Where there's a will, there's a way

Internationally, the nature and purpose of community radio are understood as primarily oriented towards ensuring democratic empowerment and societal development. The United Nations has always valued and supported community radio for its potential to deliver on UN values. UNESCO, formed in 1945 as successor to the League of Nations' International Committee on Intellectual Cooperation, promotes world peace, security, sustainable development and human rights: achievable partly by prioritizing media or press freedom, cultural diversity and, more recently, bridging the digital divide. Community radio and participatory media represent ways of doing this, so project funding is often made available from the resources yielded by compulsory and voluntary contributions from member states and organizations and private donations; a book entitled *How to do community radio* (2002) is available on their website.

There is also a profound connection with social activism. A well-documented example of this is the *"radio libre"* movement in Italy and France during the 1960s and 1970s, when hundreds of unlicensed broadcasters were "shifting the balance of communication towards civil society" (Bonini, 2014). Bonini cites the theorist Felix Guattari, referring to the creation of "the first electronic agora": a gathering place where the listeners were also the broadcasters, thereby "giving voice to sectors of society that were previously ignored" (ibid.). When eventually, the Italian state's monopoly of the airwaves was deemed illegal in 1975, the number of unlicensed broadcasters reached 300 stations within a year. King's account of the emergence of community broadcasting networks around the world suggests they spread rapidly to consolidate in an era of solidarity in the 1970s–1980s. New funding mechanisms were developed to accompany "the successful passing of supportive legislation and regulation in several countries" and the community radio movement became emblematic of the international acknowledgement of "communication as a human right" established by UNESCO's New World Information and Communication Order (NWICO) (King, 2017, pp. 24–25). This was communicated through the publication, *Many Voices, One World*, also known as the MacBride Report: the culmination of a three-year commission led by Sean MacBride with an international panel of over a dozen media influencers (MacBride, 1980).

Associations were formed for advocacy and lobbying purposes that resulted in the establishment of national regulatory frameworks, such as: Canada's Ontario Association of Campus Broadcasters in 1971; the Public Broadcasting Association of Australia (later changed to Community Broadcasting Association of Australia) in 1974; and the National Federation of Community Broadcasters in the USA in 1975 (King, 2017, p. 24). It was Australia where a community radio sector was first formally licensed in 1972 and then Canada two years later. Scandinavian countries too were ahead of the curve when "private radio licensing created non-commercial community radio stations in Sweden (1978), followed by Norway (1981) and Denmark (1983) ... in 1985, Finland introduced private licences as well, but at first only for stations supported by advertising" (ibid., pp. 25–26).

The year 1983 was a significant moment in community radio history, both internationally and for the UK. It was the year that the UK movement's representative body, the Community Radio Association (CRA), was formed. It was also the year that marked the founding in Montreal of AMARC – the *Association Mondiale Des Radiodiffuseurs Communautaires*, or World Association of Community Radio Broadcasters. Now recognized as a non-governmental organization (NGO), it promotes projects, often with financial support from other bodies such as UNESCO, tending to focus on campaigns in developing countries and disaster-torn regions. AMARC's charter begins:

> Recognising that community radio is an ideal means of fostering freedom of expression and information, the development of culture, the freedom of form and confront opinions and active participation in local life; noting that different cultures and traditions lead to diversity of forms of community radio ...[1]

Its mission also inspires academic research for development purposes: projects that are conducted in post-crisis situations, involving ethno-graphic action research (EAR) and participatory action research (PAR) intended to leave the people in those communities, participants in the studies, with the necessary skills and equipment to continue to operate the media projects on their own (for instance, Heywood, 2020).

Inevitably, there are regional variations in how these tenets are adopted around the world, but the correlation with social activism where radio is used as a tool for social change is well documented. Such "participatory communication" projects date as far back as the 1940s amongst isolated Latin American mining communities (Dagron, 2001, p. 8, 12). In his report to the Rockefeller Foundation, *Making waves:*

stories of participatory communication for social change, Alfonso Gumucio Dagron describes the first community radio station in Colombia, established in 1947 by a Catholic priest who had two objectives in mind for *Radio Sutatenza*: to deliver Christian teachings to the impoverished farming community and introduce community building skills. As Dagron points out, the number of community stations around the world has multiplied since then, and it is not even possible to state the actual quantity because many operate without legal licences (Dagron, 2001, p. 13). More recent research on radio activism in Argentina points to the continued reliance upon the medium by residents for facilitating not only the expression of local opinion but encouraging engagement in the political process over the potentially damaging ecological and environmental repercussions of processes like fracking (Serafini, 2019).

The global multiplicity of community media entities is illustrated in edited collections of work collated by leading academics in the field. Radio-specific examples can be underrepresented (for instance, Howley, 2010), but the same concepts apply. Community media is concerned with social engagement, tasked with airing alternative viewpoints, diverse and marginal voices, and facilitating enactments of citizenship, local development, social improvement and education (Rennie, 2006). Though the origins and aims may differ, it is possible to identify a general, shared understanding that motivates community media practitioners to support the rights of subcultures in society, sometimes opposing state and industry regulations. There are certain aspects that these media entities have in common and which are highly valued: being small in scale; run as grassroots organizations; prioritizing participation and community; with producers and audiences sharing the same goals (McQuail, 2010, p. 184).

The sheer scale of variation complicates theorization of the sector for making sense of local studies in a global context. In *Understanding alternative media* (2008), Bailey et al. overlay Deleuze and Guattari's rhizomatic model onto existing categorizations of alternative media to take account of the fluidity of identities between what they see as three main categories: non-confrontational community involvement; activist, counter-hegemonic; and facilitating participation in civil society (Bailey et al., 2008). In further work, one of the authors proceeds to map how these organizations are embedded within civil society, through engagement with the market and state (Carpentier et al. in Fuller, 2007, pp. 219–235; Santana and Carpentier, 2010). Nicholas Jankowski has considered how the relationship between media and community has evolved over time with technological advances

(Jankowski, 2002). He also compiled a list of general characteristics in an article, "Community media research" (Jankowski, 2003), covering all types of community media in electronic form, including radio stations. He suggests that they: share an objective of catering for, engaging and empowering local residents; strive to keep ownership and control in local hands; enable production by volunteers; serve audiences in predominantly small, geographical areas; and are financed in essentially non-commercial ways (Jankowski, 2003, p. 8). Nevertheless, there is something to be said for entrepreneurship; citizen media should not necessarily prioritize the empowerment of people for social and political gain over commercial interests (Rodriguez, 2003, p. 191 in Atton, 2008, p. 267). Alternative media requires financing and as such can be conducted as a business.

The evolution of non-mainstream radio in the UK

Community radio continues to be undervalued in the UK in comparison to mainstream media. Those who do not appreciate the benefit for people who feel marginalized sneer at the perceived amateurishness. To academics, the British version can seem mundane and banal in relation to the international sphere where helping to educate people in Africa about Ebola or reconstructing a sense of normality after conflict in places such as Palestine are a testament to the power of citizen-run radio when used as a force for good. However, COVID-19 brought into sharp relief the practical ways in which community radio stations in the UK could be relied upon in a crisis to deliver on their social gain remit. The ways in which this was achieved will be described in the following chapters, but first I present a brief history of how the sector acquired the role of primary, licensed broadcast provider of localized and special interest content. The British community radio movement seems to have diverged from its activist roots to operate according to relatively strict regulations laid out by national government and Ofcom. In order to appreciate how this came to pass, it is useful to trace the development of radio in the country from its humble beginnings in the hands of engineers and hobbyists.

Regulating the great British airwaves

Licensing for entertainment broadcasting commenced under the auspices of the Postmaster-General on behalf of the British government in 1922. The aim was to control use of the wireless spectrum to avoid frequency interference with aircraft communications and other official usage (Street, 2002, p. 19). The first licences went to the Marconi company's experimental station in Writtle, Essex, for Tuesday evenings and its other station on The Strand, London, for Tuesday and Thursday evenings (ibid., p. 21). However, the unfolding chaos on the airwaves in the USA where, by the end of 1922, there were 219 registered commercial stations, prompted a rethink. To ensure that larger wireless technology and manufacturing firms like Marconi could not achieve a market monopoly, the UK government introduced regulations so that radio broadcasting would be "for the benefit of the general public but not for the benefit of individuals" (Street, 2002, p. 27).

After some complicated wrangling between government officials, advisers and corporate representatives, the British Broadcasting Company was established to run a single broadcasting licence and produce programmes, seed funded by the larger wireless firms. Further income was to be earned from royalties on sales of authenticated wireless sets. Listeners had to register and pay to own an approved wireless set. As families across the country began to invest in the new pastime of listening to the radio, consumer demand became unmanageable. Although enthusiasts were still building their own receivers, the Post Office could not keep up with the backlog of wireless set registrations. It is not the place here to provide a detailed account of how exactly this company evolved into the BBC. Suffice to say, by 1925 a government committee decreed that listeners could buy a single licence "giving them the legal right to listen to BBC programmes" on any device (Street, 2002, p. 30). Then from 1927, having been awarded its charter from the Crown as public service broadcasting gatekeeper, the BBC took complete control, for the benefit of the listeners, over what content was produced and transmitted, with the power to determine which voices and which interests could be aired.

As the BBC grew, the preferred structure was a national system, relaying centrally made programmes across the country, with some regionalized content. From an engineering point of view, there was the capacity for localized transmissions and therefore to air more artistically and socioculturally diverse "minority" voices from different parts of the UK. Former chief engineer Peter Eckersley expressed his frustration that this did not happen in an autobiographical account of his short career with the corporation (Eckersley, 1941). He felt strongly that people from distinctive geographical regions and cultural backgrounds were not being represented. The delivery of such locally targeted programming did not happen until two decades after his departure.

This undercurrent of demand for more local representation and determination in broadcasting persisted in academia too. Sociologists at

Birmingham University's Centre for Contemporary Cultural Studies published a report, *Possibilities for local radio* in the mid-1960s (Powell, 1965). This advocated what the editors called "creative amateurism", lying somewhere between "parish-pumpery" and professionalism (ibid., p. 1). Rachel Powell criticized what she regarded as looseness and over-generality in the approach of companies who were registering interest in and lobbying for local independent radio licences. She emphasized the need for a "strong basis of local news and features of community interest" (ibid., p. 3), recommending "local-interest programmes produced locally for the locality" (ibid., p. 5).

Plans were afoot in the BBC to move with the times and restructure programming; meanwhile, competition for the airwaves continued with independent and commercially driven music radio stations on the continent such as Radio Luxembourg. Younger listeners from the UK were also drawn to Radio Caroline, which launched at sea in 1964: another threat to the BBC's control over broadcasting standards, tone, style and cultural content. These pioneering broadcasters in the English Channel were "stealing" bandwidth and profiting from playing the varieties of chart music presented by the kind of US-styled disc jockeys (DJs) denied to audiences on the BBC's terrestrial stations (Goddard, 2011). The UK government's response was heartily supported by the incumbent licensed broadcaster, especially as more pirates were emerging. A series of iterations of the Wireless Telegraphy Act of 1949 were enacted, rendering broadcasting to the country without a licence illegal. In this bid to police the airwaves, ship-based broadcasting was criminalized by the Marine Broadcasting Offences Act in August 1967.

A month later, the BBC's national entertainment and music-based Light Programme was split into Radio 2 and the popular music station BBC Radio 1, which launched with many former pirate DJs on the schedules, including Tony Blackburn and Kenny Everett, who went on to become household names. The corporation had also assigned executive Frank Gillard to explore setting up operations in every sizeable town, by installing newly developed VHF/FM transmitters and creating extra frequency space for local stations within the existing BBC network. In November 1967, the BBC launched its first local station in Leicester. Ultimately though, the number of stations was limited due to the enormous set-up costs involved (Linfoot, 2011); today there are still only 39 across England. Five years later, proponents of commercial broadcasting were rewarded with the licensing of independent local radio (ILR) stations. The Sound Broadcasting Act in 1972 outlined a public service remit in a way that was "curiously Reithian" (Street, 2002, p. 118). These operators soon found that niche local shows featuring "meaningful speech", folk music and other cultural content were not as popular with audiences as pop music (Starkey and Crisell, 2009, p. 9). Dependent as they were on building audience figures to maximize their income from both the sale of commercial airtime and Independent Broadcasting Authority (IBA) funding, this obligation was progressively relaxed over the years (Starkey and Crisell, 2009, pp. 17–18; Stoller, 2010). Ofcom's current "localness guidelines" pertaining to ILR oblige commercial operators to provide local content, conveying a sense of localness through such items as: news, travel and weather, what's-ons, interviews and phone-ins.

Pirate undercurrents

None of this provision quelled the independent-spirited alternative radio activists and popular music broadcasters. I cannot present a history of pirate radio here, but it deserves a mention for essentially being a form of community radio. It is important to note that the practice, comprising vastly disparate groups of practitioners, continues to thrive around the world. In her article "Booming at the margins" (2019), Larisa Kingston Mann considers the "strong overlap between pirate radio and radio that serves otherwise underserved linguistic, ethnic, and cultural communities" (Mann, 2019, p. 386). This suggests that on a wide scale, specific cultural interests are still not being served satisfactorily by licensed broadcasters.

In the case of the UK after 1967, pirate operators moved onto dry land and their subsequent resurgence in urban areas threatened not only to compromise reception quality for the mainstream stations but also their listening figures and therefore for the commercial stations, profit margins. This was tackled again by the passing in 1984 of The Telecommunications Act, granting investigators the power to enter properties where suspected illegal broadcasting was taking place and to seize equipment. Not all pirates closed down; the more resourceful and agile ones continued to operate. Catching them in the act was an overwhelming task for the authorities. In Northern Ireland, for instance, in "the 1980s, pirate or unlicensed radio permeated the airwaves" (King, 2017, p. 24). Such operations would again be confronted in the Broadcasting Act of 1990 which with one hand, prohibited unlicensed stations from advertising and with the other, offered them the opportunity to become legal by obtaining a licence. However, as one expert would later surmise, when discussing the surprisingly low number of African-Caribbean applicants to the government's community access scheme piloted in 2001:

the existence of numerous [urban] pirate stations may have reduced the pool of those interested in the Access Radio experiment. Also, black-led groups do not necessarily define themselves as serving the African-Caribbean community since their [music] programming can have a high degree of cross-over to white audiences".

(Everitt, 2003, p. 20)

Even today, despite Ofcom being backed by the law in operating its stern approach,[2] there is evidence on community radio social media platforms and discussion forums suggesting that licence-holders feel not enough is being done to police the airwaves and protect their transmissions from signal interference. Relationships between operators in the community radio sector and the illegal pirates are complex and strained. Though many practitioners have pirate roots, they remember well the hard-fought struggle for legitimate access to the airwaves and having won their own licence only to face continued competition from unlicensed interlopers is unwelcome. The demand for additional frequencies to be released and advertised on the spectrum has not let up. In May 2020, Ofcom announced the award of licences to six stations and in July three more, taking the total of licensed stations to around 300.[3] On both occasions, there were disappointed applicants who failed to impress for one reason or another. These groups continue to operate online therefore we have to differentiate between them and pirate radio, with whom there remain similarities in motive.

Hundreds of internet stations go about their business streaming content online in the infinite space of the web, ostensibly not inconveniencing anyone else in the process, other than competing for advertising income with the licensed local radio operators and other media content suppliers. Once the necessary technical equipment has been purchased, the ongoing costs can be manageable, though they are legally required to pay their music performance licences. These annual payments are anything from £231 for a small webcaster, to £754 plus VAT and per performance charges (0.0854 pence) for standard, commercial webcasters.[4] Some of these operators are positioning themselves to apply for mini multiplex licences in the next stage of the evolving community radio landscape with the roll-out of small-scale digital audio broadcasting (SSDAB). This innovation combining software and computer technology for low-cost broadcasting to specific geographical areas may create the promised and hoped-for opportunities for more diversity in local programming provision. A proportion of these applicants may be accommodated, however at the time of writing, it remains to be seen how the allocations will work out.

Licensing community radio in the UK

Lobbying for community access radio had rumbled under the surface throughout the 1970s and 1980s, but the regulatory framework was a long time coming. There were in-house cabled radio services for hospitals and factory floors where practitioners could train and work but the growing demand for localized wireless services could only be accommodated by short-term special event and student radio licences. In 1977, a group comprising community media activists, advocates, experimenters and creatives was established called the Community Communications Group (COMCOM) (Scifo, 2011, p. 11). Their projects included contributing to Parliamentary Select Committee deliberations and left a lasting impression on shared understandings of the mission of community radio. The defining aims were enshrined into the code of practice for the Community Radio Association (CRA) which was established at one of COMCOM's conferences in Sheffield (ibid., p. 16). These are listed in the highly regarded book *The invisible medium* and include: serving geographical communities or communities of interest; meeting listeners' needs; encouraging participation in production through the provision of training using station facilities; involving socially disadvantaged or under-represented community groups and reflecting diversity; prioritizing local or regional sources in programming; being non-profit and run by a council or committee representative of the community; and being financed possibly by a diversity of sources, including public grants, subscriptions and "limited" and "suitable" advertising (Lewis and Booth, 1989, p. 214). Long-standing campaigner, Steve Buckley, and other delegates had strong links with the international community radio movement which led to the Sheffield headquarters becoming the Western European branch of AMARC in 1993.

In 1985 it looked as though community radio was going to be introduced through an experimental scheme backed by the Conservative government's Home Secretary, Leon Brittan, whereby 21 licences across the UK for 5 km "neighbourhood" and 10 km "community interest" licences would be made available, initially for a two-year period (Scifo, 2011, pp. 19–22). For political reasons, and it was suspected also due to lobbying from the commercial sector, this project was put on hold, for fear of opposition forces getting a foothold in local media in important constituencies, such as the Labour-led seats in London (ibid.). After further to-ing and fro-ing, special event licences came into circulation which soon morphed into short term, low power, small-scale restricted service licences (RSLs) for special projects, events, hospitals, student radio and other organizations. These were often run by groups in the hope of eventually gaining a full-time licence. Then in 1989, inspired by the Thatcherist free market ideology, the IBA made provision for "incremental" licences for specific religious, ethnic and cultural audiences within geographical areas already covered by mainstream stations. This was intended as a kind of community radio provision and some pirate stations took the opportunity to legitimize their operations. However, these urban stations struggled to be commercially viable and were "forced to compromise their principles in mergers or take-overs" (Lewis, 1998, p. 5). One example is For the People (FTP) in Bristol, which was bought by the Chiltern Radio group in 1991. I was on the public relations team which successfully re-branded and launched it as Galaxy Radio, the new dance music station for younger adult listeners in the city.

As technological innovations and political manoeuvrings allowed, commercial ILR stations were increasingly administered from remote, centralized hubs and their programmes networked across several frequencies with pre-recorded split-frequency "bespoke bulletins" used for localizing reports (Crisell and Starkey in Franklin, 2006, pp. 20–21). These cost-efficiencies created regional and national networks. The Chiltern Radio network did very well initially, streamlining some of its daytime and evening output whilst maintaining local presence across several geographical locations, on both its FM (The Hot FM) and AM (SuperGold) networks. Soon though, the network became a casualty of the lifting of restrictions on ownership and was subject to a hostile takeover by a larger consortium. The implementation of The Broadcasting Act 1990 had allowed the newly formed Radio Authority to loosen its grip over operations of the ILR sector. As mergers and acquisitions ensued, the number of individual operating companies fell.

The ILRs were becoming part of big networks operating from non-local hubs, reducing the numbers of on-air presenters, newsroom staff and the delivery of localness. At the same time, the introduction of a community radio sector began to appear more likely. After a change of government, plans were set in motion for an experimental Access Radio scheme. New Labour's pilot scheme was launched in 2001, inviting applications for 15 short-term licences. These came on-air in 2002 and were deemed successful in an independent report written by Anthony Everitt that contributed to a licensing framework being put into place through the ensuing Communications Act and Community Radio Order in 2004 (Everitt, 2003). This was made possible by the gradual release of space on analogue FM and AM wavebands.

The CRA, renamed Community Media Association (CMA) in the late 1990s, in recognition of new digital opportunities, continued to provide its membership with advice and resources. It facilitated networking and later branched out into being a provider of a streaming and "listen again" service, Canstream. As a lobbying force, it engaged with the Radio Authority to contribute to the planning of the new so-called third tier of radio, although the negotiations were not, nor have they been since, plain sailing.

By 2006 after the first round of licensing, there were 107 awards and a further 184 registered expressions of interest (Hallett and Wilson, 2010, p. 11). Licences were initially for a fixed term of five years and intended for geographically delimited transmission areas reached by AM or FM frequencies: a 10 km radius for the former and 5 km for the latter. There were a handful of special interest exceptions awarded to religious, ethnic and culturally niche and specialist community stations for densely populated urban areas: a key stipulation in each organization's licence agreement being that they should contribute social gain to their target community. The sector's members were inspired in this by a speech delivered by international guest expert, Zane Ibrahim of Bush Radio, Cape Town, at the Community FM conference held in 2004. He declared: "Don't be popular. Be necessary" and when asked from the floor what the priorities involved with community radio were, he replied: "90% community, 10% radio" (Fogg et al., 2005).

Funding and sustaining the sector

The enduring business model has been very local, not-for-profit community radio stations and there are strict conditions concerning how they generate income, especially from the sale of advertising using airtime. This restriction was lobbied for by the association representing ILR to protect the commercial interests of their members and has recently been highlighted as an ongoing issue. A report conducted into the apparent neglect of community values and service by certain third tier operators has been published which ruffled feathers but reminded practitioners of the need to adhere to their legislated remits (Lloyd, 2018). Limitations on the commercial behaviour of community radio do complicate how they can generate sufficient income to keep themselves afloat. There is only a limited, static pot of funding available each year from central government, which has not risen in value with either inflation nor with the greatly increased number of stations now competing for a share in its allocation. Such precarity regarding funding occasionally makes it into the press and is inevitably a topic at the CMA events and other networking occasions and on social media.

Research into this and exploring ways in which income can be generated has been addressed in academic publications. For non-profit entities, providing the programming diversity over the airwaves which other mainstream sectors cannot or will not do, funding can be derived through an array of activities which include listener donations, grants, commercial advertising and sponsorship (Gordon, 2016). The sector's operators provide invaluable localized services across the country, delivering entertainment, information, opportunities for participatory production and media training as well as support for community projects. The benefits to society include the nurturing of contact networks and communicating useful and important knowledge to otherwise hard to reach sections of the population. One significant hurdle to be overcome before securing financial backing, is how the sector is perceived: "community radio movements have little lobbying power and are usually positioned as rogue and unprofessional actors within the broadcasting community" (Cammaerts, 2009, p. 635). There is a sense that they are looked down upon. Sitting somewhere between amateur and professional, local radio is regarded with some scorn by the mainstream and national industry operators and listeners (Powell, 1965).

Whilst there will be evidence presented later in this book that challenges the automatic assumption that community radio practitioners fall substantially short of delivering a professional service, it is true that most practitioners in the sector are voluntary. Tens of thousands of volunteers have been involved year after year, donating ten times that number of hours (Ofcom, 2015). The vast majority of them are unpaid but to describe them as un-professional would be doing them a disservice. Staffed primarily by people perceived as amateurs or as Laura Ahva describes as "in-betweeners" (Ahva, 2017, p. 143), stations are run by citizen participants, many of whom have industry experience. The community sector has access to some of the best technical minds in the industry. These not-for-profit organizations need to be operated to professional standards. Every station represents a substantial investment on the part of the multiple stakeholders and supporters, even before the licence is won. From the start, they need to have the intellectual wherewithal and knowledgeable contacts to complete the application form properly, and be able to afford the application fee which runs to several hundred pounds sterling (Fogg et al., 2005, p. 35; Ofcom, 2019a, b). Those stations awarded five-year licences, assuming they are then able to successfully launch the station on-air, find continuing operations a financially precarious and physically draining experience (Buckley, 2008). There are not only the costs of purchasing or renting and maintaining station facilities and broadcasting infrastructure, insurance, software licences and royalty payments for playing music which can reach the thousands depending on net broadcasting revenue, but there are also annual broadcast and wireless telegraphy licence fees payable to Ofcom totalling an additional several hundred pounds (Ofcom, 2017, pp. 16–17).

Filling the local news gap

The UK's community media sector and radio broadcasters are increasingly being left responsible for the provision of locally relevant, resonant and representative content: for the people, by and with the people, who have the power at their fingertips to create and share content. It is important to explore the practice to ensure that we educate and empower everyone to do so ethically, fairly and sustainably. Mainstream media institutions, especially in relation to news provision, have been restructuring in a direction that increasingly deprives localities of tailored coverage. This delocalizing of institutionalized journalism has come about as people find their lives increasingly oriented towards the national or international sphere. Yet the places where they live cannot be taken for granted; if local authorities and corporate interests are not routinely held to account, then local amenities, community resources and even residents' wellbeing may be at risk. Not every citizen is conscious that they can or should be enabled to play a role in their local public sphere. Proponents of community media do their best to facilitate the process and have taken it upon themselves to compensate for where traditional journalism is failing to serve the public. The emergence of hyperlocal journalism, practised by small teams of digital reporters across the UK, is testament to this and news for localities continues to be published on websites and in printed formats, too, where funding schemes exist. Lottery funds and charitable organizations make such projects possible and contribute to this culture of communities being encouraged and supported to provide for themselves.

In a way then, we can interpret the government policy of third tier radio in the UK as making provision for very local, independently funded, public service broadcasting. It is hotly debated in community radio circles however, whether enough is being done to nurture the sector at grassroots level: having to compete in the neoliberal marketplace with each other for funding and in some urban areas for audiences too. Ofcom responds to notifications of broadcasting and key commitment infringements and is not averse to penalizing the operators, who are subject to a five-year licence renewal process. They must aim to perform to standards that are in many ways commensurate with mainstream broadcasters, so delivering output that counts as journalistic and news-related is not without risk. Integrity is just as important in this sector as it is in larger media enterprises. They are dependent for their operations and programming largely upon volunteers who reside in the particular geographical localities: in places that really matter to them. In this sense, they are well-placed since audiences tend to look to informal information sources, people they know and therefore assume they can trust. However, there are vested interests at play, so care must be taken when relying on community practitioners for local news coverage, even when achieved largely through what I call "soft journalistic" practices. Adequate training and oversight are required to build and retain the audience's trust based on consistent accuracy of information and credibility of sources. Another primary issue to be addressed is finding workable routines for the volunteers in order to sustain their commitment, fortify the relationships and interactions relied upon to produce radio programmes and online content, and to facilitate their participation in and reporting on local happenings.

Researching local community radio stations

Critical, objective scrutiny conducted through academic research is necessary to analyse the functioning of all fields of cultural production, especially the media, because of their influential role in society. Such investigations can contribute to a range of emerging practical and policy deliberations that affect community radio: to identify the strengths and weaknesses of the sector, its future potential in the face of threats and opportunities and also what resources and actions are required to help sustain it. The following section is not only an outline of how I researched community radio stations for this study, but is intended to be a guide to researching media production practices more generally which I hope this book will encourage.

Despite the fact that community stations are performing the same practice with similar arrays of technologies and skills and sharing common aims as listed on the key commitments in their licence agreements, there are nuanced differences between them since each has its unique character. They differ according to: specific geographical location and market context; target audiences and community engagement; how they go about financing their operations; what staffing, volunteering and training arrangements they have; the nature of their programme schedules and amount of journalistic content; and other operational and output aspects. I am interested in specific instances of how digital technologies and tools can be harnessed to empower local community broadcasters. I consider the programme content which features the goings-on within a locality and which reflects and represents the views and interests of those people living and working there. I look at ways in which this is carried out: the sometimes taken-for-granted provision of musical jingles and voiced "drop-ins", identifying the station name, frequency, coverage area, taglines; live or recently pre-recorded traffic and travel or weather updates; news bulletins; what's ons; general on-air studio, phone-in (and online) discourse about community affairs; features; and interviews. I explore what influences production performances of practitioners in pursuit of their station team's over-arching purpose to deliver on their key commitments. I analyse situated instances of how they are enabled or constrained by the arrangements and infrastructures around them. My primary aim here is to consider how well the voluntary workforce in community radio is equipped in terms of technology and skills to fill the gap in local news provision by "featuring the local": covering local happenings on-air and online and through associated soft journalistic activities.

The theory behind my methodological approach

My research was planned and conducted in three phases over a seven-year period. Most recently, I conducted an online questionnaire with follow-up interviews during the COVID-19 pandemic, but this was preceded by and indeed built upon the findings of my doctoral research, written up as *Talk of the Town* (Coleman, 2020). My investigations began with desk research and listening-in, and I continued these activities throughout to keep up with the dynamic social sites I was studying. My strategy was to first undertake a creative practice-as-research project so that I could experience for myself what was entailed in producing meaningful, locally sourced content for a local audience. I knowingly applied journalistic skills and tactics in my research. I accept, too, that tacitly the embodied aptitude and attitude accrued over decades of working and freelancing in radio broadcasting continue to influence my performances of academic practice. I am in good company in media studies, especially in journalism and radio research, since so many educators and scholars have been and often continue to be active broadcasters as they conduct research into that practice (for instance McHugh, 2010; Bacon, 2012). The lessons learned in building contacts, seeking out a story, factfinding and accurate reporting can influence research conduct. The impulse to enquire, to critically analyse and to hold authorities to account motivates practitioners in both fields. Then there are the technologies commonly found in a researcher's toolkit that journalists use, including the "old" traditional as well as new digital versions, for instance: notebooks, paper versions or portable electronic devices, for writing down observations, documenting conversations and details of when and where audio or video recordings and photographs were taken (Makagon and Neumann, 2009). Other essential items include a camera, an audio or video recorder and a phone, or most often a smartphone: dubbed the ingenious 21st-century equivalent of the Swiss army knife, the device that does practically everything.

The theoretical framework I am applying is practice-centric. I use the noun "practice" to refer to the array of activities that community radio practitioners routinely engage in when playing their part in making content for their stations. I am concerned with how certain ideas and methods are applied in the way those doing it – the practitioners – usually carry out their roles. Collectively, these performances can be viewed as a field of practice. This term "field" is commonly used within and outside academia to describe different professions and indicates specialism in a specific area of interest. These everyday terms became central to the development of "practice theory" in academic circles during the last three decades of the 20th century. More a way of seeing the world than a rigid conceptual model, the practice theory approach emerged through the writings of social and cultural theorists who considered how we, as social beings with diverse motivations, transform the world around us. The perspective entails taking a position that finds the middle ground between focussing on the macro, structural aspects of society and attributing everything to human agency in an individualist way.

Two edited collections of work on practice theory have inspired my use of the approach and introduced me to a number of other academics applying the lens to study media: *The practice turn in contemporary theory* (Schatzki et al., 2001) and *Theorising media and practice* (Bräuchler and Postill, 2010). John Postill describes practice as "the work of the body" (Bräuchler and Postill, 2010, p. 11). There is a general acceptance that a practice consists of both deliberate and preconscious or automatic acts on the part of the people carrying it out, and that whilst these arrays of activities are taking place in particular contexts, they are not sealed from other practices. This approach enables me to see media production as a spatially complex set of situated practices, encompassing rather than separating out framings of media as text or content, as a technology/medium, and as a political-economic sphere. Those aspects are all part of the structural arrangements that shape and are shaped by a specific set of practices, evolving over time.

Theodore Schatzki has been developing his "social site" version of practice theory since the 1990s. I apply this conceptualization of practice-arrangements to contextualize how it is that performances are inextricably linked with the arrangements surrounding and informing them: practice unfolds according to, but also in turn influences, particular sets of circumstances and expectations, understandings, skillsets and conventions, rules and regulations. Performances depend upon the availability of and access to requisite material resources such as physical infrastructures, equipment and technologies. I theorize the influences that devices, tools and platforms have upon practitioner routines as part of the conditions and relations that enable and constrain performances of practice without necessarily giving those objects agency per se (Schatzki, 2002, pp. 42–46). Thus, I can explore the ways that media technologies are used by people actively engaged in a social, collective activity with a shared social purpose.

Studying radio production practices

Digital technologies have revolutionized the study of radio, enabling the researcher to listen intently, or as I term it "listen-in", to live output from almost anywhere. Archived audio content can be accessed at any time. Technological advances have also radically increased the potential scale, scope and speed of administrative tasks such as data searches, storage and itemized retrieval. For this research, consulting websites and publications by organizations involved in or reporting on community radio in the UK yielded useful information and statistics about the sector. As mentioned earlier in this chapter, there is a range of associations for practitioners and supporters of community radio and media which facilitate and publish what we can term "grey" literature on the field. I conducted a wider environmental analysis of what other organizations, particularly other media providers were saying about the stations, such as magazines and newspapers. A limited amount of financial information was available online through Gov.uk for Companies House if the radio stations were registered as businesses, or for the Charity Commission. Anything more detailed like turnover, salaries and budgets may be voluntarily published in reports made available on station websites, particularly if they are member-funded organizations. I found updated lists of licensees and news on licence awards, licence infringements and SSDAB matters published on Ofcom's website.

Historically, the regulator demanded annual reports from each licence holder, but this is no longer the case, so finding detailed data on specific stations was more difficult. I gleaned some limited information from updates published relating to the Community Radio Fund, where it was possible to see where funding had been awarded to which stations and for what purpose.[5] Data on target markets (age, ethnicity, locality, special interest) is publicly available information documented in each station's key commitments licence agreement and was easy to find, as was each station's transmission coverage map, by navigating the Ofcom website.[6] Estimating how many volunteers there are, allowing also for comparisons across sectors, is possible by combining those aforementioned sources and using information published online by the CMA. The body undertakes surveys, collects opinions and encourages member stations' engagement with Ofcom's public consultations. In 2015, they estimated that there were 20,000 volunteers in community radio. This compares to 13,000 people currently employed in radio broadcasting in the UK, according to research conducted by Statista.[7]

For researching specific radio stations, I engaged and immersed myself in their social media and online activities. Each had its own website with multiple pages containing, for instance: programme schedules; photograph galleries; news and information sections; blogs; contact options; and sometimes information on volunteering opportunities, membership fees and advertising rate cards. As well as listening live or listening again to shows and podcasts, I monitored listener groups on Facebook and Twitter and looked out for material posted or published by the station teams. This provided a range of experiential and subjective insights into the sound of a station, music-to-speech ratios and how much journalistic production and local news content was aired and shared online. I traced the activities and opinions of volunteers and staff, as well as contributors, listeners, advertisers and other stakeholders, such as local organizations which were subjects of on-air or online conversations. Since this approach was ethnographically oriented and required me to respect data protection and content privacy, I requested informed consent where appropriate and sought research ethics approval from my university.

Creative practice-as-research

The incentive behind using my own practice as one of the fieldwork research channels was to make the most of my innate and inculcated knowledge of audio production rather than suppress it. Designed as an auto-ethnographic exercise, this involved producing a series of audio features called *Remarkable Harpenden* for a local internet radio station in Hertfordshire. The station is no longer operational, and its website has been compromised, therefore I will not refer to it by name in this book. Every aspect of the production process, my encounters and deliberations were systematically documented on worksheets and in a journal. I inventoried the resources, devices, hardware and software used. I reflected objectively on my journalistic activities to identify practical aspects of producing local content which I could look for in the subsequent social sites I would be exploring. At the same time, I derived experiential findings that would enable me to better empathize with the ideals, instincts, moods and motivations of the community radio volunteers I would be meeting.

A reflexive mindset meant that I could account for and critically evaluate my own position in understanding the practice of others (Bourdieu and Wacquant, 1992). I was also self-conscious in my approach to the informants and the spaces within which I encountered them and observed their performances. I aimed to avoid disrupting their routines and minimize the chances of their first impressions of me unduly influencing their behaviour under observation and when answering my questions (Pink, 2008). I was mindful of my status relative to my participants, being at once an outsider as researcher, but also able to relate to them as a fellow practitioner (Etherington, 2004). I strove to remain objective and impartial in my documenting and analysis of the evidence.

Snapshot visits and participant observation

Inspired by the recent resurgence of newsroom ethnographies (Cottle, 2007), I planned visits to five additional community radio stations in market towns around England. Upon gaining research access, I noted the studios' physical locations in relation to their target audiences, their material layouts and the availability of equipment. I inventoried the devices and equipment used in the production tasks I witnessed and tried to get a sense of the intangible logistical arrangements, interdependencies and relational understandings involved. Were there common patterns of behaviour and a shared understanding of, and commitment to, the station's objective of serving the local community? I looked at the demographic profile of station memberships and the diversity of on-air voices. I considered everyone I met, and each practitioner I interviewed, as socialized through a lifetime of experiences: observing them as potentially embodying and enacting certain attitudes, beliefs and ways of doing and saying things.

Documenting my observations on a checklist enabled me to break down the everyday tasks that Schatzki terms "dispersed" activities, like talking, thinking, reading, using a phone or computer. I noted when practitioners wrote scripts, looked for sound effects and music, took or used photographs, arranged interviews, recorded and edited audio. Individual and sometimes basic tasks like those were interwoven to become more niche activities which accumulated to constitute the specialist, or "integrative", practice of producing content in ways which deliver the stated mission of a community station. I evaluated how digital technologies enabled or constrained those activities and considered how each station was structured to afford, accommodate and update those devices, software and the skills required to apply them.

Online (socially distanced) inquiry

The UK-wide lockdown in Spring 2020 was a timely intervention in my ongoing research because it provided a mutually beneficial reason to conduct an online questionnaire. It was entitled "Digital Technologies in Community Radio Production Practices: responding to COVID-19 social distancing measures", and was devised to ascertain how, and the extent to which, stations were able to successfully adapt and continue broadcasting as the crisis ensued. The findings were made publicly available for easy circulation to the community radio sector and it was hoped would provide evidence for future discussions with other stakeholders.[8] To approach all the licensed operators, I clicked my way through the alphabetical list on the Ofcom website to the radio station homepages and contact information.[9] My contacts at the CMA, the newly formed UK Community Radio Network (UKCRN) and on social media helped to publicize the questionnaire and encourage uptake. I conducted short periods of listening-in to each station's output and checked to see if their social media accounts were up to date. Of nearly 300 community stations contacted either directly by email or using "Contact Us" forms on their websites, 44 unique responses were received from stations across the UK: Northern Ireland and Scotland; the Northern regions of England; the Midlands; Greater London; the East and South East, the Isle of Wight, and the South West (See Appendix).

I sought information on aspects that included the role of the respondent in their station and whether they were involved on the presentation/production side. If so, they were asked how many shows they were normally actively involved in each week. "Normally" in this context meant prior to the social distancing measures introduced by the government in March 2020. Other information was requested about management and volunteer structures, as well as programming formats. For instance, I asked about the proportion of shows and features normally presented and transmitted live compared to those recorded from home or remote studios each week and how much that had changed under COVID-19. I was especially interested in what criteria had been applied to decide which volunteers were able to remain actively producing output, and how important it had been to maintain their usual station standards of broadcast sound quality and professionalism during the social distancing. The questionnaire also surveyed whether station teams amongst the respondents had begun to provide any new strands of programming. I was particularly interested in whether they normally provided a local news service, how it was delivered and if that had changed under lockdown. I monitored the sector's press releases, newsletters and social media posts highlighting what stakeholders and audiences could do to support their local stations,[10] and what requests might be put to DCMS and Ofcom, such as bringing forward the annual funding awards process.

Conclusion

This chapter has outlined what community radio has come to mean in relation to more general understandings about radio broadcasting worldwide. I have described the convoluted history of this third tier of radio in the UK and provided some evidence that helps to explain why the implementation of a regulatory framework was so delayed and why there are still ongoing challenges and issues regarding how the stations are expected to operate in today's neoliberal society whilst not behaving or sounding too much like their commercial cousins. I suggest this is an important reason for researching the sector, with a view to establishing what is going well, what could be done better and what provisions could be made in order to secure the continuance of radio and audio programme production which places the interests of local communities first.

I have described a mixed methods research design that encompasses: desk research including social media engagement and listening-in; auto-ethnographic practice-as-research; site visits; participant observation;

interviews; and an online questionnaire. Having established why the community sector in the UK is being increasingly depended upon to provide local news coverage and locally focussed content in affordable and sustainable ways, the terms "featuring the local" and "soft journalism" have been introduced and are discussed in more detail in the following chapters. Chapter Three presents evidence and anecdotes from the case study stations as well as a selection of their online COVID-19 survey responses where applicable. This information lays the foundations for an examination of the pivotal role played by digital tools and platforms in the lived experiences of the sourcing, shaping and sharing of locally focussed content. It will be used as evidence for considering how the digitalization of radio production affects the sociability of radio production and the interrelational nature of radio broadcasting.

Notes

1 https://amarceurope.eu/who-we-are/amarc-charter/ (accessed 19.08.20.).
2 https://www.ofcom.org.uk/spectrum/interference-enforcement/spectrum-offences/illegalbroadcast (accessed 20.08.20.).
3 https://www.ofcom.org.uk/about-ofcom/latest/media/media-releases/2020/new-community-radio-licences-in-northampton (accessed 28.08.20.)
4 https://www.ppluk.com/music-licensing/radio-tv-and-online-licensing/online-licensing/online-radio-and-services/ (accessed 20.08.20.).
5 https://www.ofcom.org.uk/tv-radio-and-on-demand/information-for-industry/radio-broadcasters/community-radio-fund/award-of-grants-2019-20-round-1 (accessed 07.08.20.)
6 http://static.ofcom.org.uk/static/radiolicensing/html/radio-stations/community/community-main.htm (accessed 30.08.20.).
7 https://www.statista.com/statistics/383593/radio-broadcasting-employment-in-the-united-kingdom-uk/ (accessed 27.09.20.).
8 https://www.brunel.ac.uk/research/Projects/UK-community-radio-responses-to-COVID-19 (accessed 07.08.020.).
9 http://static.ofcom.org.uk/static/radiolicensing/html/radio-stations/community/community-main.htm (accessed 11.07.20.)
10 https://www.theguardian.com/uk-news/2020/apr/22/uks-community-radio-stations-face-closure-as-covid-19-hits-ads (accessed 03.05.20.).

References

Ahva, L., 2017. How is participation practiced by "In-Betweeners" of journalism?. *Journal. Pract.* *11* (2–3), 142–159. 10.1080/17512786.2016.1209084.
Atton, C., 2008. Alternative and citizen journalism. In: Wahl-Jorgensen, K., Hanitzsch, T. (eds), *The Handbook of Journalism Studies*. Routledge, New York and London, 265–278.

Bacon, W., 2012. An innovative direction in academic journalism. *Pac. Journal. Rev. 18* (2), 153–165.

Bailey, O.G., Cammaerts, B., Carpentier, N., 2008. *Understanding Alternative Media: Issues in Cultural and Media Studies*. Open University Press, Maidenhead.

Bonini, T., 2014. The new role of radio and its public in the age of social network sites, *First Monday. 19* (6). 10.5210/fm.v19i6.4311.

Bourdieu, P., Wacquant, L., 1992. *An Invitation to Reflexive Sociology*. Polity Press, Chicago.

Bräuchler, B., Postill, J., 2010. *Theorising Media and Practice*. Berghahn, New York; Oxford.

Buckley, S., 2008. Community broadcasting: good practice in policy, law and regulation, in *UNESCO for World Press Freedom Day*. World Association for Community Radio Broadcasters, Mozambique.

Cammaerts, B., 2009. Community radio in the West: a legacy of struggle for survival in a state and capitalist controlled media environment. *Int. Commun. Gaz. 71* (8), 635–654.

Coleman, J.F., 2020. *Talk of the town: exploring the social site of local content production for community radio*, PhD Thesis. Birkbeck, University of London.

Cottle, S., 2007. Ethnography and news production: new(s) developments in the field. *Sociol. Compass 1* (1), 1–16. 10.1111/j.1751-9020.2007.00002.x.

Dagron, A.G., 2001. *Making Waves: Stories of Participatory Communication for Social Change. A Report to the Rockefeller Foundation*. Rockefeller Foundation, New York.

Eckersley, P.P., 1941. *The Power Behind the Microphone*. J. Cape, London.

Etherington, K., 2004. *Becoming a Reflexive Researcher: Using Ourselves in Research*. Jessica Kingsley, London.

Everitt, A., 2003. *New Voices. An Evaluation of 15 Access Radio Projects*. The Radio Authority, London.

Fogg, A., Korbel, P., Brooks, C., 2005. *Community Radio Toolkit*. Radio Regen, Manchester. Available from: http://www.communityradiotoolkit.net/.

Franklin, B., 2006. *Local Journalism and Local Media: Making the Local News*. Taylor & Francis, London.

Fuller, L.K. (ed.), 2007. *The Power of Global Community Media*. Palgrave Macmillan, New York.

Goddard, G., 2011. *KISS FM: From Radical Radio to Big Business: The Inside Story of a London Pirate Radio Station's Path To Success*. Radio Books. Available from: https://books.google.co.uk/books?id=LZ-RpGjFavoC.

Gordon, J., 2016. *How community broadcasting is funded: a useful resource for community broadcasters. 3CMedia* 8, 29–39.

Hallett, L. and Wilson, D., 2010. Community radio: collaboration and regulation, in *Media Policy & Regulation. Current Challenges, Radio Regulation & Policy. MeCCSA Annual Conference*, LSE, London.

Heywood, E., 2020. Radio journalism and women's empowerment in Niger, *Journal. Stud., 21*, 1–19. 10.1080/1461670X.2020.1745668.

Howley, K. (ed.), 2010. *Understanding Community Media.* SAGE Publications, London.

Jankowski, N.W., 2002. Creating community with media: history, theories and scientific investigations. In: Lievrouw, L.A., Livingstone, S. (eds), *Handbook of New Media: Social Shaping and Consequences of ICTs* (first ed.). SAGE Publications, pp. 34–49. 10.4135/9781848608245.

Jankowski, N.W., 2003. Community media research: a quest for theoretically-grounded models. *Javn. Public 10* (1), 5–14.

King, G., 2017. History of struggle: The global story of community broadcasting practices, or a brief history of community radio. *Westminst. Pap. Commun. Cult. 12* (2), 18–36. 10.16997/wpcc.227.

Lewis, P.M., 1998. Radio theory and community radio. In: *Meeting 3: Theory and Methodology in Local Radio and Television Section.* Local Radio and Television Section, IAMCR, Glasgow.

Lewis, P.M., Booth, J., 1989. Serving neighbourhood and nation: British local radio, in *The Invisible Medium: Public, Commercial and Community Radio.* Macmillan Education, London, 89–114. 10.1007/978-1-349-19984-6_6.

Linfoot, M., 2011. *A history of BBC local radio in England c. 1960–1980.* PhD Thesis. University of Westminster.

Lloyd, D., 2018. *Small-scale Radio in the UK. How Local Commercial and Community Radio Can Co-exist.* Radiocentre. Available from: https://www. radiocentre.org/wp-content/uploads/2018/11/SMALL-SCALE-RADIO-IN-THE-UK-ONLINE.pdf.

MacBride, S., 1980. *Many Voices, One World: Towards a New More Just and More Efficient World Information and Communication Order.* UNESCO, International Commission for the Study of Communication Problems. Available from: http://digitallibrary.un.org/record/80 (accessed 20.09.20.).

Makagon, D., Neumann, M., 2009. *Recording Culture: Audio Documentary and the Ethnographic Experience.* SAGE Publications, Thousand Oaks, USA.

Mann, L.K., 2019. Booming at the margins: ethnic radio, intimacy, and nonlinear innovation in media. *Int. J. Commun. 13*, 383–401.

McHugh, S., 2010. *Oral history and the radio documentary/feature: intersections and synergies.* PhD Thesis. University of Wollongong. Available from: https://ro.uow.edu.au/theses/3255.

McQuail, D., 2010. *McQuail's Mass Communication Theory* (sixth ed.). SAGE Publications, Los Angeles, CA; London.

Ofcom, 2015. *10 Years of Community Radio in the UK.* https://www.ofcom.org.uk /about-ofcom/latest/features-and-news. Ofcom, London. Available from: http:// consumers.ofcom.org.uk/news/community-radio-at-10/ (accessed 12.05.15.).

Ofcom, 2017. *Notes of Guidance for Community Radio Licence Applicants and Licensees.* Ofcom, London. Available from: https://www.ofcom.org.uk/__data/ assets/pdf_file/0016/101860/Community-radio-guidance.pdf (accessed 01.09.19).

Ofcom, 2019a. *Community Radio,* Ofcom, London. Available from: https://www. ofcom.org.uk/manage-your-licence/radio-broadcast-licensing/community-radio (accessed 08.09.20.).

Ofcom, 2019b. *Ofcom Tariff Tables 2019/20,* Ofcom, London. Available from: https://www.ofcom.org.uk/__data/assets/pdf_file/0032/141899/tariff-tables-2019-20.pdf (accessed 08.08.20).

Pink, S., 2008. An urban tour: the sensory sociality of ethnographic placemaking. *Ethnography 9* (2), 175–196. 10.1177/1466138108089467.

Powell, R., 1965. *Possibilities for Local Radio.* Centre for Contemporary Cultural Studies, Birmingham University, Birmingham.

Rennie, E., 2006. *Community Media: A Global Introduction.* Rowman & Littlefield, Lanham, MD.

Santana, M., Carpentier, N., 2010. Mapping the rhizome: organizational and informational networks of two Brussels alternative radio stations. *Telemat. Inform. 27* (2), 162–176. 10.1016/j.tele.2009.07.003.

Schatzki, T.R., 2002. *The Site of the Social: A Philosophical Account of the Constitution of Social Life and Change.* Pennsylvania State University Press, University Park.

Schatzki, T.R., Cetina, K.K., von Savigny, E. (eds), 2001. *The Practice Turn in Contemporary Theory.* Routledge, London; New York.

Scifo, S., 2011. *The origins and development of community radio in Britain under New Labour (1997–2007).* PhD Thesis. University of Westminster.

Serafini, P., 2019. Community radio as a space of care: an ecofeminist perspective on media production in environmental conflicts. *Int. J. Commun. 13* https://ijoc.org/index.php/ijoc/article/view/11524.

Starkey, G., Crisell, A., 2009. *Radio Journalism.* SAGE Publications, London.

Stoller, T., 2010. *Sounds of Your Life: The Rise and Fall of Independent Radio in the UK.* John Libbey, New Barnet.

Street, S., 2002. *A Concise History of British Radio, 1922–2002.* Kelly Publications, Tiverton.

3 Sites and sounds of community radio

Introduction

This chapter presents insights and information from research studies conducted between 2014 and 2020 to explore specific situated examples of how practitioners produced localized content for community radio (see Appendix). First, I recount my own practice for a local internet station, both as a radio reporter and academic researcher, and how digital technologies enhanced my capacity to source and process information. I then describe the performances of practitioners I encountered during fieldwork implemented through snapshot visits, interviews and participant observation at other community radio stations. I also present some findings of my online research inquiry conducted during the COVID-19 pandemic, designed to establish how stations adjusted to the lockdown and which devices and software facilitated their ongoing operations. It is important to bear in mind that the practitioners whom I describe participating in media production and journalistic activities were unpaid volunteers: citizens whose contributions represent the interwoven nature of local radio with the communities served (Atton, 2008; Ahva, 2017).

Home-produced local content for a hubless virtual radio station

I found out that there was a local internet radio station for the town where I lived, Harpenden, in 2013, soon after a small group of experienced community radio practitioners had launched it. Their aim was to establish a solid listenership and a good reputation with local organizations in readiness for applying to Ofcom for a licence, as and when one associated with a frequency for the locality became available. There was no actual studio building; it existed as a club with a bank account and a few committee members. The former website for the station (now defunct) had several pages of local information and clicking on the "play" icon on the homepage enabled the output to be streamed. Alternatively, the station could be found on various streaming services like TuneIn. In its early days, there were 15 named presenters on the programme schedule, producing music-based shows remotely using their own equipment in home studios. Only half of the team lived or worked in the local area, the other shows were nationally or globally syndicated shows by presenters such as UK-based Sean Bell and Mark Gale and USA-based Tom Fallon. Pre-recorded audio packages in MP3 format were transferred using file share services such as Dropbox or sent through the mail on memory sticks so that the volunteer programme director could upload them to the playlist schedules on his computer, by "dragging and dropping" directly into the station's playout system "RadioDJ".

Consequently, most of these shows were neither locally produced nor locally focussed, and nothing went out live. Prior to my research internship with the station in 2017, I had occasionally reported from local events such as political hustings, festivals and theatre productions: recording interviews which I then edited, topped and tailed and emailed to the scheduler. Only one other volunteer was making local programmes. Sylvia, also the station's fundraising and public relations person, presented an hour-long rock music show that played out twice a week and *About Harpenden*, an hour of music with local interviews, repeated six times a week. Her home studio was located ten miles outside Harpenden, comprising: two computers, a mixer, two microphones, two CD players, turntable, amplifier, and a radio. She described working her way around the table and a shelf. After editing each show and saving it as an MP3, she would give the file its required name and upload it to the station's Dropbox account so that the system could automatically load it into the right places on the schedule.

She recorded conversations with people over the phone about forthcoming local events and schemes, although she had also negotiated use of the Mayor's parlour at the council offices to conduct interviews using a small handheld audio recorder or the electronic notebook with a pair of microphones which the council had helped to fund. She engaged enthusiastically with local businesses and charities, attended and promoted local events and was very active on Twitter. As she was the only volunteer doing this sort of public interaction, she told me she felt synonymous with the station in the minds of the audience. Sylvia talked emotionally with me about experiencing that certain:

...feel good factor ... with the community programme – you know I interviewed Helping Hands, Harpenden Trust, the Lions, the Round Table, all these people. And they all do so much for their community and globally as well, and it's just giving them a platform.

I decided to create a series of speech-based features to inject more locally sourced and focussed content, designed to be repeatable and useful schedule fillers. I wanted to help generate audience engagement for the station and build its reputation as a local media provider. I collected printed matter such as newspaper clippings, council brochures and publicity flyers, and I searched the internet on my computer for information on websites and social media to track down potential contributors. I stored these details in document folders in the cloud, which meant I could access them on my smartphone or tablet, when thinking through options while away from my desk. I liaised regularly over the phone and by email with my informant, who helped run the station from his studio in a spare bedroom of his suburban home. After agreeing on a title, *Remarkable Harpenden*, I drew up a list of ideas for topics which would reflect the history, culture and environment of the town. I approached people to interview: most were already acquaintances of mine, but one or two I tracked down through Facebook and via email or contact forms on websites. Once their participation was agreed, I emailed them information and consent forms, exchanged phone numbers and arranged to meet them for interview. One contributor who ran a busy corner store, was dealt with face-to-face and with hard copies of the paperwork.

All interviews were carried out on location, in homes or workplaces and on two occasions outdoors. I was equipped with my "Handy Recorder" H4n manufactured by Zoom Corporation (not to be confused with Zoom Video Communications). I also had my smartphone with pre-loaded "Voice Recorder" software and a downloaded app for broadcastable recordings, "WavePad Free". Relying on handheld devices meant I could be mobile, but I had to keep an eye on the battery life and available memory. I tried to avoid recording in poor sonic conditions such as inclement wet or windy weather and noise-polluted locations where machinery was being operated in the vicinity, such as diggers and lawnmowers. Even indoors, I encountered telephones ringing, creaky furniture, loudly ticking clocks and unexpected interruptions. I timed the interviews in my home for during school hours to avoid potential hubbub from my family and hoped my pets did not cause any disturbance or set off allergic reactions in my participants.

I recorded two gardeners on the town's allotments on a cold, damp Sunday afternoon. We had met in the adjacent church car park at the hall where a boisterous children's party was taking place. The main road was busy, which meant that my microphone picked up plenty of unwelcome sounds as we walked around the plots talking about the allotment lifestyle. I attempted to stay close, keeping the microphone near the mouth of whoever was speaking. Editing the interview down to create the impression of a seamless conversational narrative in an idyllic countryside setting was challenging and time-consuming in post-production. Fortunately, I had also recorded wild track from a nearby locality on a quieter occasion, including cheerful bird song which I was able to insert to cover any obvious inconsistencies in the underlying traffic flow. As well as recording natural sounds from every place I visited, I took photographs depicting the aspects of Harpenden that my contributors discussed. I used my digital camera for its higher quality images as well as my smartphone, which was also handy for accessing Facebook and Twitter, sending and receiving emails, and occasionally searching the internet whilst in the field.

With 13 audio interviews in the can, I set about the post-production to shape the material into ten features. I did this in my home study on the desktop computer. All the audio recorded on my portable recorder was uploaded directly in the standard format of waveform audio files (WAV), by inserting the Zoom's digital memory card into the reader. I directly connected my smartphone to copy across the raw audio files. I transcribed and timecoded each interview so that I could use key term and phrase searches when storyboarding narratives for each feature. This was time-consuming; it took me five minutes to transcribe one minute of audio (industry standard is 4:1). Each hour of audio, which was the average length of my recordings, took five hours to do. I was not aware at the time of any reliable, free software that I could have used for this purpose but have since learned of various artificial intelligence (AI) and automatic speech recognition (ASR) programs that automatically transcribe speech to text, such as YouTube's built-in captioning and Otter. Basic, free accounts tend to set monthly limits on the number of minutes you can have transcribed, which would not have been sufficient for the amount of audio I had. Of course, there was also the option of commissioning a professional to transcribe, but the texts would still require checking through for accuracy. I preferred to trust my own ears, save money and maximize the amount of exposure I had to the material I was working with.

This immersion made subsequent revisiting of over 13 hours of interview material, for building themes and narrative threads, much easier and facilitated writing the blogs and tagging the topics, place names, events and contributors for the social media publicity posts I was planning. The themes that arose and around which I shaped the ten episodes ranged from the history of the nearby international agricultural research centre to the social life of the local allotments club, and from charitable good causes like the food bank to the voracious demand for residential building plots. I storyboarded each feature using tables in Microsoft Word, so that I could copy and paste then edit paragraphs of time-coded transcriptions until I had more or less finalized the structure of each piece, prior to copying the corresponding audio segments into the working file. I edited using Audacity, free open source, broadcast-standard software. I saved as I went along in the cloud linked to my computer and backed everything up on a portable hard drive. I generally used headphones for accuracy, but when each feature was near completion, I also tested listening to the audio playing in the background whilst doing housework or some other activity, as is customary in much audience consumption.

The completed features were exported as MP3s and I filled in the metadata providing details: myself as contributing artist (producer), the name of the track (for instance "Green Fingers") and album title (*Remarkable Harpenden*), year, genre and length. I then sent them one by one or in pairs by email, capacity allowing: the average file size being 13 MB. The maximum file size I could send using my Yahoo email was around 30 MB. I also delivered the collection in bulk on a memory stick by hand. I requested that they be introduced one at a time to the schedules and hoped they would remain online for several months.

Scheduling issues

My informant arranged for the features to be scheduled for regular but random playout; however, there were some initial problems that had more to do with a technician's manual error than the technology. When each feature was uploaded into a given hour of programming, it was not taken into account that my audio packages, averaging at eight minutes duration, were longer than the usual music tracks, so inadequate space was made for them by removing existing items. This resulted in the features being routinely "dumped" automatically by the computer programme. I had told my contributors to listen out for them, so when I began to receive emails and texts saying no one had heard any, I made a phone call to my informant. Initially, he was confident that we were somehow missing the transmissions. However, as he and I sat through a 15-minute window whilst, at his end, he watched the scheduler progress into a new hour on the screen in front of him, it became apparent that he needed to "force play" rather than rely on the system.

The programme scheduler eventually managed to rectify this "fault", and my contributors were able to hear *Remarkable Harpenden* features if they committed to listening to the station for long periods of time. I also took control of making the audio available myself by posting the features onto my free Mixcloud account with a link to them from a blog, which I created especially for the project using a basic account on the open source publishing platform, WordPress. I publicized both these virtual places where my audio features were available using tags and photographs on my Facebook and Twitter social media accounts.

Despite my efforts to create content about the local area, contributed and voiced by local people in order to generate a more local sound on the station and potentially increase listenership, the station did not thrive. The production process had involved my active engagement in the community, meeting and interviewing people which helped raise the station's public profile a little. To capitalize on this short-term project over the longer term would have required the station's members to follow up and build on the awareness and the links that had been formed. Their failure to do this was largely due to the fact that there was no social hub for the station, very few locally based volunteers and little programme-related liaison or even socializing between them. Sylvia left the group in 2018 to join a different community station elsewhere. After her departure, re-runs of my *Remarkable Harpenden* features became the flagship local content on the schedule. By Spring 2019, mentions of anything local were minimal: just on commercials, community announcements, trailers and station idents. Within another six months, the station had ceased broadcasting.

Producing content and building community at local stations

During 2018, I paid one-off visits to the studio hubs of four community radio stations to conduct interviews with managing directors, staff and volunteers. I also listened-in and researched their websites and social media to glean further information. Below are outlined first the findings from 103 The Eye and Vibe 107.6 FM. Then I cover the snapshot studies at Somer Valley FM and Radio LaB, whose managers also took part in the online questionnaire I conducted in June 2020, enabling comparison of their responses from before and during the COVID-19 crisis. I proceed to describe and discuss a longer term study of another station, Radio Verulam, which likewise features in my lockdown research.

103 The Eye – station base and family home

103 The Eye, licensed for Melton Mowbray in rural Leicestershire, was the first station to launch on-air after licences were first awarded in 2005. The station was based at the licensees' house situated a short distance from the town centre, on a tree-lined residential road. It comprised a room between the kitchen and a small conservatory overlooking the back garden. The owners, couple Christine and Patrick, maintained this small well-equipped studio, with several screens each with a keyboard and one control panel spread out along a waist-high, half-hexagonal desk, three large microphones, three guest chairs and an adjustable office chair for the presenter. There was one dedicated phone line into the station and one handset. If a show was being presented from a volunteer's remote studio, then the line would be diverted there. This ensured that elderly and less physically active volunteers could produce and present material from the comfort of their studies or spare rooms doubling up as satellite studios. About 10–12 shows were routinely pre-recorded weekly and sent via the internet so that Christine could load them up into the automatic playout system. One presenter preferred to send his shows on a memory stick. The programme schedule featured some high-profile syndicated shows to supplement their output, such as the *Sixties Vinyl Countdown* with Roger Day, Mark Stafford with *Stafford's World* and *Live Wire* on selected evenings. Their key commitments required a weekly provision of 70 hours of original content; 13 hours a day had to be produced locally.

Christine had a background in journalism; so as well as being managing director and coordinating the programme schedule and volunteers, she routinely arranged interviews for the station's flagship Sunday morning local news show, presented by Patrick. If unable to attend in person on the Sunday, the guests would be allocated to other presenters during the week. Then Christine would "edit the more interesting interviews", take out the music and insert them into the playlist to be repeated on Sunday mornings. She explained: "Speech-based programming is much more labour-intensive and difficult to produce than just bunging a few songs on". Patrick added: "People join the community radio stations and they all want to do the presenting music side of it. Very rarely do you get anybody come along who wants to do the news gathering side". So it was often left down to them to attend local events looking for opportunities to record interviews on their Zoom and a back-up memo voice recorder.

Christine was also responsible for compiling the "what's ons" each week, a pre-recorded read-through of forthcoming events in the local area. Presenters were expected to play that feature and also to refer to local and national newspapers, hard copies or online, for stories, as well as keep an eye out on websites and social media for interesting things going on in their locality. There was a public Facebook group where presenters posted promotional messages about the station and engaged with listeners, and they were also part of their own online, private Facebook group, which helped to encourage the family atmosphere with Christine and Patrick in charge, as relatively liberal "parents". Through this platform, the 60 or so presenters and other volunteers and contributors offered each other friendly advice and moral support, heartily welcomed new members with friendly emojis and animated stickers, and shared show or event updates. They posted photographs and videos of themselves interviewing guests in studios, reporting from events and entertaining crowds from their roadshow trailer at local fairs, races and carnivals. The Eye's website looked old-fashioned and static in comparison but carried information about the station and target area: photographs of local sites of interest and activities that presenters had been involved with; the programme schedule; event listings; and information on how to advertise. A link to the "listen live" stream was on their home page and broadcast output was also available on TuneIn and similar platforms.

I observed in progress the live Saturday sports programme with a young stand-in presenter filling in for their usual host. He masterfully combined digital and printed sources to deliver conversational updates to his audience: match facts; current form; recent results. These were delivered between music tracks and live reports and he spared time to talk me through the procedures. He described pre-recording interviews for the programme with players, football managers and coaches, often visiting their clubs to do so. While speaking to me, he kept an eye on the screen for social media updates on matches. Results from different clubs were posted on Twitter and Facebook and the show had its own dedicated Twitter account. Sometimes the studio phone was used for receiving reports from places like West Bridgford, the City Ground where Nottingham Forest played. Another computer screen was for national sports updates by Sky reporters for Independent Radio News (IRN), filing reports from grounds further afield and the final scores. If he chose to, he could fade across to take this news feed live, or he would record a report off-air and edit clips if necessary, for later transmission during the show.

Attention to timing was crucial. In the last half hour, I watched the presenter take two IRN feeds of match reports, including the classified results "down the line". Heading towards Sky News at the top of the hour, he also had to allow enough time for the weather update in his countdown. He then handed the studio over to Christine and she lined up a remote feed to the live programme due to follow, which was being broadcast from a presenter's remote studio near Leicester streamed through a standalone encoder into The Eye's desk using a service such as Shoutcast. The station's only voice-tracked show played out later on Saturday nights, the *Melton Top Ten*: a 40-minute show which Christine put together using links pre-recorded at the station on Fridays by a volunteer who lived two streets away.

Having the studio to themselves on Saturday evenings allowed Christine and Patrick time to prepare for the Sunday morning programme, load up any other pre-recorded content and do a general tidy up. This also gave Patrick the opportunity to make his weekly check on all the equipment, which was a necessity to reduce the number of technical glitches that might arise. For instance, a problem with the computer, a router or any cabling might risk the connection to the internet or the transmitter dropping, which could cause disruption and dead air until fixed. Because the main studio was in Christine and Patrick's home, they were always on hand to react promptly. They always tried to deal with technical problems themselves and had even been known to go out to investigate their transmission site in the middle of the night in the snow. No one at the station received payment for their time. Only external services, like accountancy and engineering in case of a more complex breakdown of the transmitter, were paid for.

Vibe 107.6 FM – high-tech studio and training centre

The community station for Watford, located northwest of London within the M25, was quite a contrast to The Eye. Vibe 107.6 FM competed with the capital's mainstream music stations for a youthful target market, and several managers were paid, albeit on a part-time basis. It was licensed to provide at least eight hours of original programming, live or voice-tracked to sound live, and a minimum of 13 hours a day of output produced locally within its transmission area. Based on the second floor of local government offices housing other community service organizations and charities, Vibe was a professional set-up in a spacious, light-filled open-plan office with two good-sized studios, a rack room and kitchenette. At the time of my visit, the station team were just completing a major overhaul, fitting state-of-the-art touch screen technology, the "Zetta" playout system, and adjustable console desks with stools to allow presenters to stand whilst working on their shows. The chairman, Howard, explained that the new equipment would provide the volunteers with a more contemporary industry experience of radio broadcasting. One young presenter in his mid-twenties, a graduate in multimedia journalism, told me: "I always found that once you've done it, it's kind of like riding a bike ... once you've worked on one desk, you can kind of figure out others in different places".

Another new piece of kit was a phone system that monitored calls coming into the studio. Station protocol when listeners phoned in to enter competitions or contribute to on-air proceedings was to record conversations off-air and edit them before broadcasting. Quick, easy digital editing software replaced the traditional, industry-wide seven second delay adjustment, or "profanity button", that safeguards against anything libellous or profane being broadcast (Fleming, 2010, p. 149). Funding for Vibe's new studio equipment was sourced through council and lottery grants and awards, and Howard was hoping to sell their old analogue gear to another community station to raise money to invest in a new piece of software, such as Adobe Audition editing software and associated licences. Going digital also meant being "plug and play", so the station team would have more flexibility if they ever needed to downsize or relocate the studios. Howard indicated that he also hoped to purchase equipment to do outside broadcasts (OBs) from places around the area, instead of relying on phoned-in reports back to the studio or recording on-location interviews for later transmission. Their strategy in the meantime, was to cover and create community happenings by livestreaming and videoing publicity stunts from the town centre to post online and talk about on-air.

Howard envisaged equipping the station so that presenters would have everything they needed on a laptop in order to record remotely and send their content to the station for transmission. There was clearly sufficient expertise amongst the station team, with young, tech-savvy volunteers on board. One programming assistant/producer, interested in broadcast engineering, said he had learned a great deal from helping with the studio refit alongside an experienced industry professional. The process had given the younger volunteer confidence and a reassurance that in the future, he too would be: "happy going in and pulling cables out and knowing what to do". The studio consoles could be controlled remotely so it was possible for someone to fix technical issues from home, whether that was a local volunteer or the engineer himself who lived a two to three hours' drive away and apparently never charged Vibe full price for his time. There was also an

IT specialist who lived locally and occasionally helped out, and it was not unheard of for the programme controller to be called out of bed at seven on a Sunday morning to fix system breakdowns at the station. Sounding good on-air required all the volunteers knowing how to treat the equipment correctly; a disruption might simply involve a damaged microphone or mistakenly switching off the wrong computer.

Listening-in to the station, I was impressed by the professionalism of the team, comprising around 30, mostly young presenters. Though many of them voice-tracked their shows, it was not obvious. The technology meant they could be flexible and much more efficient in their working arrangements. A volunteer could prepare an entire three-hour show in just one hour or less, on a day and at a time to suit them, up to a week and a half in advance. This meant that their involvement with the station was not dependent upon, or constrained by, their availability for the actual timeslot they were allocated on the programme schedule. Using the spare Studio 2, without compromising live transmissions, they could log into the system and pre-record a series of tightly timed personalized links and chat, continuity updates and introductions to music tracks that were then uploaded into the playlist and checked by the programming team before playout.

Unless voice-tracking was done the night before, the localized traffic and weather reports would not be covered. This meant that the prime breakfast and drivetime shows had to be broadcast live. On breakfast, the presenter routinely invited listeners to call the station phone or even his personal mobile with traffic updates. He trusted his regular callers, but other more formal sources were available on websites operated by organizations such as London transport and the airports, apps such as Google Maps and industry providers of traffic data like "INRIX", using satellite navigation systems fitted into motor cars and commercial vehicles. As for weather reports, a range of websites or apps could be consulted, and the IRN newswire provided updates and forecasts. Other on-air mentions of the local area were achieved through station idents, local advert breaks, presenters discussing localities as part of their broadcast chatter.

There were volunteers who took a more journalistic approach to their content provision and several ardently followed local sport especially football. For instance, throughout the week, the Friday drivetime presenter would keep a constant eye on social media and local newspaper websites, *The Watford Observer* and the St Albans and Hemel Hempstead papers. If there was an interesting story, he researched it further and would create a document on his laptop for notes, names and web addresses. Each week, he took a print-out with him into the studio. He described himself as old-fashioned for relying on sheets of paper, though I suggested that this was still considered best practice in professional circles. The station's part-time, paid programme controller was always on hand for those volunteers who did not have the confidence to identify newsworthy stories. He would source local news items and national stories with local resonance from Twitter, local and national newspapers, hard copies and websites. He checked details, wrote up and passed on the material for the presenters to use in their shows. National news bulletins on the hour were supplied by Sky News for IRN, and like many stations in the UK, Vibe used the company's net newsroom for sourcing other sport and entertainment news.

The station's multipage, dynamic website was a key element in its news offering to Watford, with a portal to local, sports, national, entertainment, business, weather and other news articles and links. Even when transmitting voice-tracked shows, the presenters scheduled social media posts in advance to run alongside, enabling online engagement to appear live. The listen again facility for the station's output was limited to podcasts of radio interviews with local sports people and celebrities visiting the area and was also used to showcase recordings from the specialist music show, *Raw Vibes*. This was an opportunity for performers from Watford and North London starting out on their music careers and looking for exposure. The show was usually broadcast live. I was told band performances and their interviews were sometimes videoed and received thousands of hits on social media.

Somer Valley 97.5 FM – community hub for educational training

Similar to Vibe, a primary mission behind Somer Valley FM (SVFM) was to deliver training opportunities through the operation of a community radio station. In this case, the emphasis was not on producing the next generation of professional broadcasters but on developing general employability and media skills for young people, and for adults with autism or Asperger's. The station had launched online in 2008 in association with the area's schools and technical colleges, generating local support which helped towards winning the Ofcom licence. Since 2009, it was simulcast on the internet and FM to a rural population of around 70,000 in the former mining communities of Midsomer Norton and Radstock in Somerset. When I visited in early 2018 to interview station manager Dom, I learned that the station was also part of the Ofcom pilot scheme for small-scale digital licences, which extended its reach up to 15 miles away to Bristol and Keynsham.

As chairman of the Community Media Association (CMA), Dom had been one of the architects of the Memorandum of Understanding with the British Broadcasting Corporation's (BBC) English Regions local radio network, creating opportunities for mutual cooperation, news sharing and mentorship. He had professional experience of working in newsrooms for the BBC and commercial networks, so as well as leading the training at SVFM, he produced daily news bulletins himself and occasionally recorded interviews for the daytime schedule. Dom also presented a weekly music programme and was volunteer coordinator and station manager. For running the station, handling airtime sales and funding applications, ensuring that it stayed solvent and adhered to safeguarding guidelines and risk assessment and so forth, he and an assistant were both paid and reported to a board of directors. The station's key commitments to its audience included the provision of 70 hours of original programming each week, at least 13 hours a day produced locally. Music output was a mix of easy listening, chart music and some specialist genres and speech content including news and sport, local information, discussion and arts features.

A contract with educational charity The Somer Valley Education Trust, was a primary source of income for the station. It involved providing experience in a range of communication and media skills. This meant that the trainees produced content for the station. At the time of my visit, Dom said they were running three projects for a pre-apprenticeship scheme with nearby Bath College, whereby trainees spent three or four days a week at the station. Each morning at 9:30 am, trainees would start the day by looking online for local news stories from second-hand sources like local newspapers and the BBC website. After selecting stories, they typed up scripts for two-minute news bulletins typically comprising three items plus a weather update, which they then recorded in the production studio. Trainees followed the same process with compiling what's ons and sometimes interviews. Before being aired, Dom said the work would be cleared for compliance with the Broadcasting Code and with the traditions of news broadcasting, such as the contributors namechecking themselves.

There was a sizeable training and production studio for this activity on the ground floor of the studio block which was situated in a light and airy two-storey building at one of the secondary schools in Midsomer Norton. There was also a small kitchen, accessible toilet and reception room. Upstairs were the rack rooms, a small sales office and two further studios either side of a soundproofed window. Each studio had a wooden table adapted to hold a mid-sized control panel with three mics, computer with keyboard and a monitor for the playout system. In the larger studio there was also space for a small round table. This could be used for recording panel discussions and workshopping with trainees or volunteers, or if removed there would be space for choirs and bands to perform. The volunteer body numbered between 61 and 80 members producing between five and seven different shows each day, almost three quarters of which were usually broadcast live and mostly from the radio studios.

SVFM had a contemporary and informative website, but their Facebook page was their principal outlet for public engagement online. With a direct link to Twitter too, this made communicating with the presenters much easier for listeners. Even though there was still a telephone number for the studio, rarely any calls came through and the text service was no longer used. Presenters shared media with their listeners: posting selfies and video clips recorded on smartphones. They showed themselves in action in the studio and promoted their shows by posting longer clips of guest interviews and live music performances. Videos posted indicated the range of events that station volunteers participated in or reported from such as fairs, markets and other social or business functions including election result announcements. Dom explained how posting a message about a forthcoming theme for a particular show would generate engagement. He gave an example of listeners sharing suggestions for appropriate song titles: 50 or 60 contributions on any one thread of conversation was not unusual. "It's about hitting a resonance" he said. "That's what we're doing in radio anyway. We're social media, we're trying to engage our audience to participate cos community radio's really the voice that empowers a community".

Dom was the first to respond to the online questionnaire that I circulated in the COVID-19 survey. He said that his active involvement under social distancing measures had increased a lot; he was spending many more than his usual 21–30 hours a week on station matters. He said they were "excellently resourced, [we] had everything we needed to proceed" and explained that they had been able to utilize all three studios in order to introduce good social distancing practices. He was able to continue managing the station from his office, which was physically isolated, and when necessary he could remotely manage operations in the studios. Their technical manager, a professional broadcast engineer with commercial radio, was overseeing everything remotely and advised on good practices of hygiene and studio use in compliance with government guidelines. Dom was one of the 15.9% of respondents who said that they had achieved a marked increase in the number of shows being produced each week under lockdown. He reported that there had been a slight increase in speech content and that live broadcasting had increased a lot with many more than the usual handful of practitioners presenting remotely from home. They had been able to set up any vulnerable volunteers for home broadcasting within ten days of the lockdown coming into place. Normally speech accounted for between 10% and 25% of output, but since lockdown, they had added news bulletins to two-hour live breakfast shows, one hour at lunch time and another two hours on the live afternoon shows, Monday through to Friday.

Radio LaB 97.1 FM – campus-based community station

Another station I visited to conduct interviews was the student-led community station Radio LaB 97.1 FM. Dating back to 1997, it was first launched as Luton FM, a restricted service licence (RSL) initiated by academic and community radio advocate Janey Gordon (2000). The recently re-housed and modernized studios were based on the ground floor of the University of Bedfordshire's Luton town centre campus. A small suite of offices comprised an administrative area with desk space for three people on computers with large monitors suitable for audio editing, a spacious cubicle comfortably seating three around a radio desk, a smaller production cubicle and a larger studio for round table discussions or performances. There were large windows in the soundproofed partition walls between the studios and looking out onto a university courtyard.

Radio LaB was licensed to provide a minimum of 13 hours of locally produced output each day, and at least ten hours of that had to be original during term times, or at least four hours during vacations. The station also served people over the age of 55 and had non-student volunteers from the town helping to achieve the key commitments of facilitating discussion and the expression of opinion to increase mutual understandings and strengthen links within the community (Ofcom, 2017). Music-wise, the station offered a variety of alternative and specialist genres. Volunteers were able to plug their phones or laptops into the desks through aux leads if they wanted to play music tracks not in the station's playlist collection, or on CD or vinyl. They hosted musicians and recorded live performances to post online on Facebook. The station's dedicated local music show was presented by a non-student volunteer, who DJ'ed as "Rebelyous" and enjoyed access to a wealth of multicultural talent. He would pre-record batches of editions of his *HOH Show* for transmission on Monday evenings. The show opened with the jingle "Your Luton, your music", followed by drop-ins in multiple languages before launching into an upbeat mix of urban music, live performances and conversation.

Station coordinator, Terry, was responsible each year for recruiting four new student managers to operate the station as their final degree project. Their roles included building relations with local organizations, dealing with fellow student members, and liaising with the volunteers from town. Terry circulated studio guidebooks and other station information by email but since students tended not to check their emails, Terry would communicate news and updates via WhatsApp and a private Facebook group. The public website was quite small, with a few pages of basic information, but there were links to the built-in media player service from Canstream and to Radio LaB's social media accounts: Instagram, Snapchat and Twitter with around 3,000 followers at that time in 2018. The volunteers were encouraged to post online whilst they were broadcasting and there was a tablet in each broadcast studio, already logged on to those accounts. They were asked to sign and agree to conform to the station's social media policy, to ensure that they did not post anything even on their own social media accounts which might reflect badly on the station.

Under Terry's supervision, students dealt with the University's press department for leads on potential stories and also with the university's journalism department. The station hosted News Days as part of The Broadcast Journalism Training Council (BJTC) accredited courses for broadcast journalism students. These students would experience going live on-air by linking up from their training studios to Radio LaB and presenting their final bulletins. Although the department had an IRN subscription for students to practise using the feeds and taking audio clips, the Radio LaB team did not take the hourly bulletins since historically, it was not something they had deemed important. I interviewed one of the student managers who was interested in journalism. He did four shows a week, one of which, *Luton Buzz,* covered topical stories gleaned from press releases, local press and news websites and Facebook. He conducted "feel-good interviews" covering items like charitable good deeds, upcoming events and wildlife rescues which he referred to as "soft news". The half-hour show he put together with the student recruits he was helping to train would include a round-up of "all the big news stories … what's going on in the government". Past projects included coverage of elections and a National Health Service (NHS) blood donor campaign involving on-location interviews and reporting using an OB kit.

This student treated his role at the station as a job, working six days a week. He usually recorded his own shows at home using a professional quality Razer Seiren microphone into Audition on his computer, editing as necessary before uploading to Microsoft Onedrive then into the Myriad cart for scheduled broadcast. Doing the production at home meant that it was easier to edit as he went along. A self-confessed perfectionist, he pre-recorded in sections so that he could check for mistakes and redo bits if necessary. He could also pre-record in Team Viewer using his smartphone, but the quality was not as good. Terry also had access to the station's Team Viewer account which enabled remote access to the studio system, so he could resolve certain technical issues without physically being at the station. Assuming he had internet access, Terry would be able to log in at weekends wherever he was on a smartphone or computer.

When the lockdown occurred, Terry was one of only a small number of University staff on a list of people allowed to enter the building upon request. He immediately went in to check the studios were in order and applied some settings to facilitate remote technical operation. He explained:

> I put the off-air studio fader up in the on-air studio just in case something went wrong with the on-air studio, so we could use the off-air studio and just broadcast from there … And using our OB kit as well, I made sure that was ready to go. Should we ever find a reason to do an outside broadcast.

There were normally more than 40 student volunteers and between six and ten regulars from the local area including a group of 16- and 17-year-olds who produced and presented the *Youth Network* show. Terry had asked everyone to do what they could to continue broadcasting during lockdown, but only a few responded positively, many "dropped off radar completely", and he was left with a skeleton programme schedule. Of the townsfolk, the oldest volunteer, a rock'n'roll fan in his 70s, continued with his routine. He was, according to Terry, "ahead of the curve" in already using a USB microphone and Audacity to pre-record his Sunday morning music show. The station had adequate resources for live remote broadcasting using browser-based audio-conferencing service Cleanfeed. However, some of the students found the experience unsettling and were not happy with their programmes, preferring to pre-record whole shows from home instead. For Terry, the priority was to provide audio, even if the sound quality was compromised. For instance, he was comfortable with the students using music downloaded from the Radio LaB system by WeTransfer, then editing it into a solid one- or two-hour show on their own computers. They then exported and uploaded that content back up to the playout system.

Voice-tracking was limited anyway because Terry found that their Myriad software was not effective and required updating.

Being accustomed to the annual turnover of student volunteers, Terry was used to taking over programme production during the summer months but would normally be assisted by students back in Luton from other universities, which was not happening because the station was off-limits. Fortunately, one of the student managers about to graduate with a broadcast journalism degree, had stayed on to produce a weekly news spot, reporting and recording interviews on topics such as Ramadan, student accommodation and other university issues. A new strand of on-air programming was a series of interviews with university staff. Another initiative had come about when the annual High Town Festival in Luton was cancelled. The organizers approached the station to find a virtual solution. Radio LaB was used as a platform for their *Radio Takeover Show* which featured music performances from previous years and special lockdown performances by musicians who had been prevented from participating in person.

Despite this new content, Terry admitted that he would struggle to meet the station's key commitments in terms of hours and hoped that being honest with Ofcom would elicit their understanding of the situation. He felt that they were essentially still broadcasting from the studio, with pre-recorded shows, public service announcements and mental health features going out amidst automated music. "That's one of the eye-opening things", he said. "All of a sudden, you see that now we maybe should have done more about this beforehand. And so that's why we need to make sure we act on it when we can, now". Indeed, Terry and the new student managers had been spurred on by the challenges posed by COVID-19 to update station protocols and implement a "brand reboot". The team was planning to change aspects of the station's online presence, and the students were thinking of producing podcasts for on-air broadcast. Terry had started experimenting with an Alexa skill, enabling the schedule to be uploaded so that when asking for Radio LaB, Amazon's app would welcome the listener to a particular, named presenter's show. Everyone knew they would be doing things differently heading into the next academic year with so many unknowns and contingencies ahead. Freshers Week and Freshers Fayre would potentially be virtual, so planning for how Radio LaB was going to be a part of that and how they would get around the university to recruit volunteers would change. Having experience in making radio programmes and innovating approaches to running the station under those conditions would usefully inform the students' future professional practice.

Radio Verulam 92.6 FM – local station and online hub

Research into the sixth station, Radio Verulam (Verulam) involved a four-month long participant observation study in 2018. Two decades earlier, I had volunteered with the station, presenting both weekday and weekend shows over a five-year period. I had kept in touch with one of the founders, phoning the studio occasionally to promote local societies and deliver local news reports. Much had changed since the early days when we transmitted on the Telecential cable TV Channel 10 from an industrial estate in Hemel Hempstead, then began webcasting from makeshift studios above shops on a nearby high street. Since winning the licence for 92.6 FM in 2006, the team had moved to St Albans. Spending time in close proximity with them would enable me to develop a keen appreciation of how the station had progressed and to observe the significance of digital technologies in volunteers' production routines.

I conducted a pilot recce of the station in 2015. The studios were located on the first floor above a café in a Victorian building close to the St Albans city railway station. There was a small Radio Verulam logoed sign on the front of the building where access was possible when the café was open and there was another entrance at the rear from a small carpark. At the top of a narrow staircase was a security-coded door that led along a short corridor, lined on one side with a handful of chairs, into a small office area with a desk, a computer, telephone and some office storage. There was a single roof light in the ceiling. There was no rack room. Instead, electrical equipment for monitoring, modulating, encoding and sending studio outputs to the transmitter on top of a nearby church tower, was stacked on a small mezzanine platform above the smaller of two studios. A large, soundproofed window offered a view from the office desk into that studio, which had a second window into the larger Studio B.

The smaller Studio A accommodated two people side by side at a mixer deck, each with their own microphone. There were two computer monitors, each with a keyboard. Both studios had carpet lined walls, a radio-controlled analogue clock, on-air, "mic live" and phone indicator lights, speakers bracketed to the wall, an air conditioning unit, a CD deck with USB sockets and a telephone on the console. The larger Studio B had three monitors, the spare one being for a contributor or producer to use. There were four large microphones on angled stands. Four people plus the presenter could comfortably be seated, although, when I helped with International Women's Day, we accommodated eight. Of the two screens facing the presenter's seat, one was for Myriad, the station's playout and automated scheduling software, referred to by the presenters as "the system". The other was connected to the internet for browsing the web and calling up documents from Verulam's shared repository in Google Drive. The control desks glinted with rows of knobs and indicator lights, columns of number-marked faders and colour-coded labels. There was space in the centre for a keyboard and mouse as well as for a laptop, tablet or smartphone and, as some presenters preferred, printouts or pads of paper.

Coverage of local current affairs

According to director Clive who wrote the initial licence application for Verulam: "Originally and basically we're here to help people become broadcasters and learn radio techniques". The station's key commitments required 91 hours of locally produced material each week, at least 40 hours had to be original. Thus, there was a constant demand for content. Coverage of local topics and happenings seemed to happen organically on most shows, even those that did not feature interviews or studio discussions. This was because the presenters would often chat between music tracks about their recent experiences and share word-of-mouth news picked up as they carried out their daily lives in and around the locality. The volunteers monitored emails and press releases directed to the station as well as the internet and social media to both search for ideas and potential guests as well as to connect with listeners and promote their shows. They had learned to build up lists of well-connected contacts and reliable information sources and regularly engaged contributors in what can be termed "civic news talk" (Hutchby, 2001, p. 482). They seamlessly incorporated non-digital media in their work, for instance many presenters were carrying folders of press clippings, magazines, flyers and publicity brochures to read from and refer to during their shows. They used printouts of what was lined up for their programmes or handwritten preparation notes when conducting interviews.

The station's subscription to IRN's Sky News was a reliable online resource for national or international news and features of interest including celebrity gossip and sports updates. Where presenters had producers or studio assistants, they delegated to them the task of writing up and reading stories on-air. Not all the volunteers considered such fact-finding, interviewing, writing up and sharing of information as journalistic. Rather, they were motivated to come across as plugged in to the local community, so it was in a presenter's interest to get involved, connected, keeping their ear to the ground and eyes peeled for who was doing what locally: be that fund-raising schemes, arts and crafts shows or festivals, awareness campaigns and so forth.

There was a local news-focussed current affairs programme, *Outspoken,* which appeared on the schedules from time to time, when a suitably confident and competent volunteer was available. I interviewed one who was a businesswoman and former local government councillor. She had covered topics such the rail freight interchange issue by interviewing politicians and corporate representatives and encouraging listeners to phone in and comment on-air. Having only one phone line though was a hindrance. "Interacting with the audience is great", she told me, "but you have to have the technical facilities". Another show she produced and presented was a magazine-style evening series, *Days of Our Lives.* Planning ahead, she would research online to compile a list of themes which were topical but not as time-sensitive, using local news websites including the BBC. Sometimes, she selected national issues but always looked for a local angle. She arranged to interview expert guests such as a doctor, travel consultant, security adviser or gardener, either where they worked with her portable recorder or in a Verulam studio. With an eye on efficiency, she would record several weeks' worth of short interviews on different topics with each contributor. She edited to tidy up the interviews where necessary and uploaded each segment to the system. At home, she would script her introductions and narrative around each contributor's piece, and then book more studio time to piece together each hour-long edition of the programme into the allocated carts on the system, playing in the recorded audio at the appropriate points.

Another speech-based topical series I observed being pre-recorded was *Environment Matters,* produced and presented by a local environmentalist. Broadcast as part of the weekly *Local Life* evening programme, it was then made available on the station's website and on podcast platforms such as Spotify, iTunes, TuneIn and Stitcher. With catchy single sentence titles indicating the subject matter and the date they were originally broadcast, the podcasts were identifiable by eye-catching images: logos, posters and photographs of featured guests. Another by-product of the show was a blog on the station's website which followed ongoing stories and promoted events such as fund-raisers, exhibitions and campaigns. The presenter was a local Green Party member and an active campaigner on Twitter and Facebook, so there was clearly a cross-over between her personal life and her radio volunteering. Through social connections, she had her finger on the pulse of local sustainability, recycling and ecology-related issues as well as global issues with local implications, like climate change. In preparation for her shows, she would look for news on seasonal activities by reading articles published in the press, magazines and online, and collecting campaign leaflets and brochures. She sought the opinions of residents as well as high profile experts to whom she enjoyed privileged access. Correspondence and invitations to interview were usually sent using email and followed up by a phone call. She prepared scripts in word documents on her computer at home and emailed questions to the guests just before their appointment.

Routinely she booked the smaller studio for an hour one afternoon at the beginning of every week. The day I observed her in action, she had cycled to the station and wasted no time setting up at the console with a folder of information sheets and flyers and her laptop. She received one guest who arrived promptly for a face-to-face interview and then conducted a further interview over the station's only studio phone line routed through the desk. Each discussion segment lasted around four minutes and was recorded "as-live", saved into a coded cart on the system, ready to be inserted into the final edited version of that week's 15-minute episode. She listened back to the interviews whilst working on her laptop to finalize her script for the remaining six minutes of the show, which would include her introduction, links to the two interviews and mentions of forthcoming activities in the local area. She took a couple of goes recording herself before being satisfied with her delivery, admitting she was hypercritical of her own work: always the perfectionist but at the same time frustrated by that. It also meant that she ran over her allotted time in the studio that day, and a fellow volunteer was impatiently waiting to get in.

Pre-recording content

Studio bookings were organized via the station's intranet. I observed that it was fairly common for Verulam's presenters to pre-record their shows. Of the sample of 23 practitioners I interviewed from a pool of around 60, seven of them working on five shows routinely time-shifted the delivery of that content. They made concerted efforts to sound live whilst doing so. Some even simulated real-time engagement by making dedications for listeners, running competitions and so forth. For those volunteers who preferred or needed to use station resources for pre-recording, it was beneficial to have the flexibility in their working week to be able to book a spare studio to suit their timetable. Clive and a student mentee used to record their two 28-minute segments into Myriad from Studio B every Wednesday morning. They had a two-hour slot from 11 am, preceded by a drink in the café downstairs to plan what they would be talking about.

Several presenters pre-recorded their shows remotely because they had access to broadcast-quality equipment at home or elsewhere. I observed and interviewed one experienced presenter who had a soundproofed studio booth in his garage. This arrangement meant that he could fit volunteering at the station around his full-time work, other interests and his young family. His approach was to record as if he was broadcasting live, mainly because he could not allow himself the time to redo things. He said: "It's not gonna work if I'm thinking: 'Oh, oops, I'm going to go back and just do that again'". His method for a two-hour weekend show was to record six 18-minute segments of chat and music tracks and upload the entire show into Dropbox. The system then played them out at the scheduled time and the listeners were none the wiser, unless, he admitted, all the technology went wrong. I did also once hear him get some facts wrong which exposed the ploy. He was not up to speed on station news and launched into his show by thanking the outgoing presenter for her entertaining programme and teasing her about the luxurious purple sofa she had squeezed into the studio. In fact, the presenter in question was away that week and another volunteer had filled in for her: a man with a very different voice and style, who did not mention any sofa, imagined or otherwise.

The team was expected to keep abreast of station news using the virtual message board on the shared Google Drive. This repository was a source of "coming up later announcements" or CULAs, intended for producers to post what they were planning to cover in their programmes. These were useful fillers when a presenter needed to find something to talk about in order to segue neatly into an advert break, or to meet the strictly-timed countdown to the news on the hour. Another useful source of local material was the user-friendly Community Noticeboard, a calendar designed for listeners and other stakeholders in the area to provide details of their forthcoming events and booking information. Verulam's well-designed and information-packed website went on to win Silver in the "Innovation" category of the 2019 Community Radio Awards.

Many presenters used social media platforms to promote their shows and were comfortable streaming from the studio on Facebook Live and Instagram. This self-publicity was important for maintaining their profiles and helping promote their guests' interests. Studio assistants would share live or recorded footage of interviews and even musical performances online. Participating in such live engagement made it possible to track hits, likes, downloads and shares. Gauging listener reactions to different outputs was important for estimating audience numbers, demographics and potentially their geographical distribution which helped with valuing airtime so that advertisements and sponsorship could be sold. Stations do not always have the luxury of pursuing what idealists yearn for: an uncommercialized existence (Gazi and Bonini, 2018).

Voice-tracking

The more seasoned presenters could also voice-track their music-based shows. It was routine for the breakfast show presenter on her weekday early morning slot to record short links, traffic and weather updates for the first hour or two from home. This meant that she and her regular contributors did not have to be in the live studio until the more sociable hour of 8 am. Other presenters preferred to voice-track at the radio station because the studio microphones produced a better sound, and they preferred the atmosphere. When I later interviewed the volunteer programme controller as part of the follow up to my COVID-19 questionnaire, he described his voice-tracking set-up at home in a spare room: a basic laptop borrowed from the station, and a Samsung G track USB microphone. With Myriad, he could upload his own material to the server but also had access to check the logs and scheduled content as required.

He explained that for his weekly two-hour 1980s music show, he normally spent half an hour planning the tracks and logging on through a different system to sort out the structure of his playlist. Then if he was "feeling really efficient and alert" he would only need about 25 minutes to log into the voice-tracking system and record all the links. If he were not having such a good day, or was having a problem with the computer, it could take 45 minutes to an hour. That was still much less time than he would have spent at the radio station and travelling there and back. He described the versatility of being able to either stick to a standard ten-second link or stretch it out to talk for 50 seconds instead. A running total would be displayed showing how far along the hour he was, indicating what needed to be added or removed, and even the time each link would be aired. He did have his reservations though, commenting that the process did not have the soul of live radio. When asked to explain, he replied:

> The reason why you're doing a music programme is because it's your music, that you're into. That means you know all the facts about it, all the stupid anecdotes, the memories it creates … When

it's live, you have each three-minute song to think about what those things are ... and when you push that microphone open, you can be genuine. 'Oh, that was great. I remember when this happened, I was at this place here...!' And it's all very natural. When you've just got a list of all the songs and you're just doing a link every two or three songs, you almost have to force those memories. It's easier with practice, but you don't have the same connection because you're just going to plonk, plonk, plonk ... you can't script it ... there's no passion.

Live shows

One of the most popular live shows I studied on Verulam was *The Parents Show*, broadcast every Thursday evening. The core team communicated with each other via email and held monthly production meetings to forward plan each week's topics and who they would contact for interviews. Between them as working mothers, they had connections with organizations such as the local schools' alliance, national agencies dealing with child-related matters, academia, and media development programmes. They would phone experts and contributors to book for an interview. Running orders were created on Google Docs and scripts were printed out onto A4 paper to use during the broadcasts. Lists of questions would be shared with interviewees a week in advance; 40% of interviews were by phone or occasionally Skype, and 60% took place at the station, in the larger Studio B. One presenter explained:

> It's pure laziness on my part, it's just that I have that slot carved out and it's just live, just suits me so much better. Cos I feel like I'm doing the job twice if I go and hire a studio and go in and do a pre-record.

The team felt that the pre-recording process would be too time-consuming administratively, and it also might involve editing on Audacity, which they did not enjoy doing and claimed not to have the technical capability. The other presenter admitted:

> In an ideal world, I wouldn't touch the mixing desk ... I'm a massive fan of outsourcing ... doing everything is exhausting and really nerve-wracking and it's just a personal decision that it's not my thing. I don't want to do it.

Although they aimed to localize their content covering themes relating to education and parenting, they had listeners and followers from far beyond the target area and often interviewed internationally renowned experts. They shared material online to promote upcoming shows, using topic hashtags and asking the audience for contributions, suggestions and questions to pose to guests coming in to the studios. Facebook groups and pages, like local mums' and parents' networks, helped to not only amplify their voice and encourage the continuation of conversations started on-air, but to generate new ones and source fresh content. A wealth of photographs, videos, hyperlinks to other websites and podcasts, clipped, topped and tailed from their shows, were posted after each transmission. When I met them, they were in the process of recruiting a volunteer for technical support. They needed a replacement for the local parent who had been expertly producing their podcasts: "You need someone who pays attention to detail", they explained. Their hope was to train up local sixth formers in his place.

Another successful team effort and the most complex live speech-based show on the station was *Verulam Sport*. For three hours each Saturday afternoon, the headline presenter aimed to deliver all the latest sports news. He would usually arrive at the station an hour before going to air to schedule calls and record reports with several correspondents from various grounds across the country. During my observations, I noticed that he used his smartphone to check first that these roving reporters were in position. To record their scene-setting pieces, he called them again using the studio phone connected into Audacity. With his contact at Watford Football Club for instance, he worked his way through three scripted questions, starting with Watford's poor form and ending with her confirmation that she would phone through updates later. Happy with the interview, the presenter saved it with a five-digit code and uploaded it straight into the system, overwriting the existing audio in the destination file. He then went through the rest of the playlist checking that refreshed carts were in the correct allotted time slots and removing music to allow for the reports and interviews to follow.

During the show, a studio assistant was contact point for their regular correspondents, who were an assortment of fans, coaches and commentators from Old Albanians rugby club, Watford and London Colney football clubs and the local netball league. The assistant had their details and the anticipated times they would call on an A4 printout, as well as a list of any studio guests that had been booked in. Whenever she had a caller waiting on the phone, she slipped quietly into the studio so as not to disrupt the on-air flow, and waved a folded piece of paper displaying the guest's name until the show host acknowledged her, changed conversational tack and prepared to take the call. Leaving nothing to chance, he relied heavily on his smartphone, texting reporters to check on their availability and constantly checking Twitter for updates and feeds from and relating to local clubs and games.

On the main studio computer, the presenter had access to IRN's Sky Sports news service for national and international updates, match summaries and live reports from the grounds, sometimes downloading their reporters' audio to play out. He dealt skilfully with the organized chaos that live sports reporting inevitably involves. Although he had timetabled every phone-in report, he expected last minute changes which meant being flexible with when he could play out other pre-recorded interviews such as with local sportsmen and women, club executives, charity promoters, campaign leaders, even authors of sport-related books. He needed fillers such as notes on that day's matches with extra bits and pieces for potential talking points. Local newspapers such as the *Herts Advertiser* were used to source content as well as the occasional press release about forthcoming events and campaigns. Thus, he was prepared with plenty of material to fill time, in case anyone in his tight schedule let him down or if the playout system went down; while it was rebooting, he would be able to keep talking. Every now and then he would declare on-air: "It's your show, contact us", reminding listeners of the ways they could get involved: "Call, text, tweet, email!" Although as he pointed out to me, there was only a single phone line. "You don't really want listeners phoning", he admitted, "when your reporters are supposed to be calling in!"

So successful was this formula, that the team had won Silver in the 2017 Community Radio Awards "Sports Show of the Year" category for live coverage of St Albans versus Carlisle United in the Football Association (FA) Cup, and were awarded Silver again in 2019. The station had a close relationship with neighbouring St Albans City Football Club since two of the station's presenters were announcers at the ground, and the correspondent who usually covered "The Saints" was matchday organizer there. This connection with players, management and supporters allowed them privileged access to information enhancing the station's credibility. I interviewed this Saints reporter about his other contributions to the show, especially how he sourced and shared other local sports information.

Reporting and outside broadcasts

The Saints correspondent had been involved with Verulam since retiring several years earlier. He recalled trying to set up a results-reporting system directly with a range of local sports clubs which had not been successful, although he had gradually built up a network of contacts. He was thankful for social media and the internet, because it meant that he did not have to rely on the printed versions of local newspapers' retrospective accounts, which would have made his sports news a week out of date. He was able to use online message boards for eyewitness accounts and Twitter feeds of sports clubs and the *Herts Advertiser* online sports pages as his main sources, as well as *The Non-league Paper*. On Saturdays, he would phone in to deliver St Albans' match reports, from the ground a short distance away or from another stadium in England, having driven there with the away fans. On Sundays, at home in his living room, he would spend 40 minutes recording a short round-up of all the weekend's results to upload to the system for the following week.

To file his live match reports from St Albans Saints games, he sometimes used Luci Live on a borrowed station smartphone. This software was an internet protocol (IP-based) app for use with a laptop and USB microphone or a smartphone with high processor power. However, he confessed to preferring his standard mobile phone which he found more straightforward. It is still the case that to look professional and to capitalize on a visible presence for promotional purposes, stations like Verulam have a radio car of some description, sometimes purchased second hand from local BBC stations. I know this from personal experience and research intelligence, since OBs are under researched in radio studies receiving only passing mentions (for instance: Starkey, 2011, p. 76; McLeish and Link, 2016, p. 254). Verulam's OB manager aimed to have a vehicle bearing station branding at a range of important events through the year, such as the annual Hertfordshire County Show. This booking involved the station team broadcasting six hours a day from the event site over the last weekend of May. There were usually ten station volunteers on a rota with two presenters for each two-hour slot, a technical crew, reporters and producers to edit the reports.

As part of my research, I attended a few lower-key events that had been promoted on-air and online by Verulam and from which live reports were being broadcast. At the annual pancake race in the St Albans marketplace, I watched the crew attempting to use Luci Live to connect with the studio for off-air talkback and on-air two-ways. They were hoping to create their own Wi-Fi hotspot converted from the 4G mobile network via a gadget they described as a modem. The gear was set up inside the chairman's saloon car parked alongside the race track, decked out with a laptop and microphone, with arrays of speakers around the bonnet and on the roof rack for making announcements and playing out the station's transmission or background music. Unfortunately, there was insufficient mobile data available in the crowded city centre at that time to produce a strong enough connection. Instead the reporters resorted to phoning the studio with their updates.

Teamwork and training

When issues with technology are severe enough to disrupt a broadcast, there must always be a back-up. In Verulam's case, there was a fader in the studio that brought up its automated music player. During my observations, I witnessed several instances when things in the studio went wrong. The computer and the Myriad system were not always 100% dependable, although often human error and simple mistakes would be involved. I was in Studio B one afternoon during *Drivetime* and another volunteer who had been listening at home phoned in to say we had gone off air. It turned out the presenter had forgotten to return the studio to live mode after he had taken the opportunity during a couple of back-to-back tracks to pre-record a voice link for later in the show. Clearly, it was important not to panic when there was a problem; the whole system could freeze or "crash" if a presenter made too many commands too quickly or pressed a wrong button. There might be another volunteer in the station who could help, or a station director like the programme controller would be contactable by phone. He would be expected to talk them through what needed to be done, or remotely check the system and make the necessary adjustments at his end to restore the live broadcast. This protocol caused tension though and one director commented: "There's more than a little bit of presumption about, 'Well, you're on the board. Clearly you don't have a life!'".

There were several director-level members at Verulam with professional experience or media training expertise such as BBC technical staff, consultants from the telecoms industry, graduates and educators in media studies. Volunteers with experience and the aptitude to be trained were highly valued; the dream team would include someone capable of working with the more complex background technology, the aerial and FM transmitter, because paying for experts was a drain on the station's limited resources.

At the time of my research, the station management was introducing a new training programme. Volunteers had to attend workshops and update their accreditation for certain skills like presentation. One initiative was a critical listening scheme using a system called "Snoop" which enabled voice-tracked samples to be selected and studied in order to survey, evaluate and learn techniques from other radio stations. This was causing friction; some people I spoke to resented being expected to spend more time and money on attending the sessions when all they wanted was to continue doing their own show, in their own time and in their own way. For the station's chairman, cooperation was crucial and he was determined to improve the level of engagement. With compliance to broadcasting standards being such an important aspect of any licensed station's performance, training was deemed vital yet clearly under-valued by those that should have been undertaking it.

Lockdown response

In his role as a director, Clive completed the online questionnaire in my COVID-19 survey. He recounted the steps they took to maintain on-air delivery of the usual programmes wherever possible, after they made the decision to close the studios. From my time spent at the station, I could readily picture how impossible it would have been to devise a rota of studio usage and deep cleaning and I could easily imagine the frustration of those volunteers who felt excluded as a result. Where there were normally around 70 volunteers producing about 50 shows per week, this number reduced dramatically to between 10 and 12. This meant that for a small crisis team of volunteer practitioners, selected with the aim of maintaining professional standards, the workload increased dramatically.

The station had good IT facilities enabling volunteers to broadcast from home, but less than ten of them had routinely produced and pre-recorded their shows from home before lockdown and knew how to voice-track. Thus, less than half (between 25% and 50%) of the content being broadcast sounded the same as usual. There was a marked increase in the amount of speech programming. Before lockdown, this accounted for less than a quarter of all output. Since then, the team had introduced on-air coverage of local news within magazine shows and online on their website and social media. They were fortunate in that an experienced journalist was already on hand. Her paid, part-time administrative role coordinating Verulam's volunteers had ended, but she stayed on as reporter. More content from the *Talking Newspaper* service was also incorporated into programme schedules and their usual evening slot was expanded to two hours and repeated weekly.

As time passed, other regular presenters were encouraged to start contributing recorded features and interviews. In the follow-up interview I conducted with the programme controller, he explained that this number had gradually grown to around 30 people after some one-to-one training sessions over the web-conferencing platform, Zoom. But there was a capacity limit with the remote voice-tracking kit. Because it was based on a server at their studios, only one person could log in and use it at any one time. On the day we spoke, the controller checked the bookings and there was not a free hour between seven in the morning and eight at night. He explained that reliability was essential, as was whether the volunteers were disciplined enough to manage the tasks themselves without needing "loads of hand-holding" for which there was no capacity. He added:

> I think we're putting out more local now than we ever have ... people have discovered new ways of working in new software and realized the benefits ... there's also people who have been trying out new things [outside their comfort zone] that we wouldn't normally be able to accommodate. And I think that's really good ... at the other end, there are some people who are totally disengaged and just gone.

Conclusion

A wealth of information and insights has been presented in this chapter illustrating the ways in which practitioners apply their skills and knowledge to perform their roles in local community radio, according to certain understandings, protocols and conventions established in their local contexts. It has also demonstrated the repercussions for practice from changes in the availability of tools and technologies and in the conditions and physical environment wherein it takes place. Having performed the practice myself as part of the research process meant that I could more readily identify the tasks and activities involved in producing local content and associate them with particular technologies. This provided me with a heightened awareness of what evidence to look for in those other social sites as well as a sensibility for noticing the nuanced impacts and influences that one's surroundings and arrangements have on the production of content.

In the following chapter, I contextualize and consider further these findings against additional evidence and insights gleaned from the COVID-19 research project. As my discussion of the material unfolds, I distil what it all means in relation to how radio station operations are understood. Through the framing and mindset I introduced previously, we can construct an understanding of how digital technologies are implicated in their practice-arrangements. We can begin to appreciate how practitioners are differentially equipped or skilled to perform within the evolving circumstances of contemporary broadcasting and to respond to an unexpected crisis and potential turning point such as the lockdown.

References

Ahva, L., 2017. How is participation practiced by "in-betweeners" of journalism? *Journal. Pract. 11* (2–3), 142–159. 10.1080/17512786.2016.1209084.

Atton, C., 2008. Alternative and citizen journalism. In: Wahl-Jorgensen, K., Hanitzsch, T. (eds), *The Handbook of Journalism Studies*. Routledge, New York; London, 265–278.

Fleming, C., 2010. *The Radio Handbook*. Routledge, London.

Gazi, A., Bonini, T., 2018. "Haptically mediated" radio listening and its commodification: the remediation of radio through digital mobile devices. *J. Radio Audio Media 25* (1), 109–125. 10.1080/19376529.2017.1377203.

Gordon, J., 2000. *The RSL: Ultra Local Radio*. University of Luton Press, Luton.

Hutchby, I., 2001. "Witnessing": The use of first-hand knowledge in legitimating lay opinions on talk radio. *Discourse Studies 3* (4), 481–497. https://doi.org/10.1177/1461445601003004009.

McLeish, R., Link, J., 2016. *Radio Production*. Focal Press, New York; London.

Ofcom, 2017. *Notes of Guidance for Community Radio Licence Applicants and Licensees*. Ofcom, London, UK. Available from: https://www.ofcom.org.uk/__data/assets/pdf_file/0016/101860/Community-radio-guidance.pdf.

Starkey, G., 2011. *Local Radio, Going Global*. Palgrave Macmillan, Basingstoke, UK. Available from: https://books.google.co.uk/books?id=4yV-DAAAQBAJ.

4 Practitioners and content production

Introduction

In this chapter, I explore further how the practice of producing local content unfolds in specific station contexts. Through this social site framing (Schatzki, 2002), I can identify how the employment of digital technologies enables practitioners to carry out their roles according to shared understandings of a purpose as they navigate other influencing arrangements amid their station. Insights yielded from desk research and fieldwork discussed in the previous chapter are distilled and contextualized against findings from an online survey I conducted during the COVID-19 crisis. The aim of this latter project was to ascertain how licensed stations were faring in terms of programming and production under lockdown and social distancing (Coleman, 2020).

First, I consider the physical environments of the different stations I visited. Traditionally, a radio station is a building or suite of rooms containing a number of studios, offices and at least one reception area accessible to the public. This convention developed over time as the institutionalization of broadcasting ensued. But is it now becoming an anachronism? Taken for granted in academic literature as context for newsroom ethnographies (see for instance, Cottle and Ashton, 1999; Hemmingway, 2008), the material attributes of an actual "station" are rarely explored. Katie Moylan's assembled approach to studying community station structures, practices and content is a welcome contribution especially for her community radio focus (Moylan, 2019). I then shift my attention to the virtual dimension and look at radio stations' online spaces, accessible to audiences as digital community hubs and consider how those were utilized for achieving social gain objectives. This leads to a discussion of how the continuing developments and innovations relating to digital technology impact upon production. I break down how the participants in my study sourced, stored, shaped and shared local content for their target audiences. The meaning of the term "soft journalism" in this context will become clear as I describe how they delivered coverage of news and views relevant and meaningful to their listeners. I focus then on whether their target communities were represented effectively in station output and if diversity was reflected in their volunteer membership. I also analyse my survey findings for what the data suggest about how well the sector achieves diversity in pursuing its collective purpose of locally based provision of localized media content.

I proceed to reflect on how digital technologies were used to maintain operations and sustain the production of local content under COVID-19 conditions. Practitioner performances were compromised when factors beyond their control interceded so that they could no longer access the physical studio hubs in the ways they were accustomed. The working arrangements of many stations were stripped back to become essentially hubless operations, and practitioners were either prevented from meeting face-to-face or intentionally avoided physical encounters with each other. The sector faced the challenge of ensuring the continuation of communications between management, practitioners, contributors and other stakeholders by building on existing links, connections and relationships. I suggest that the fact operators appear to be surviving indicates that this licensed third tier of community radio has come of age.

The radio station as a place for community

Ofcom is clearly wise to the technological feasibility of remote broadcasting and so it stipulates on each individualized key commitments document that: "The studio is located within the licensed coverage area". A station must be situated somewhere that content can be "mostly locally produced" and should be "creating direct links with its listeners, offering training opportunities and making sure that members of the community can take part in how the station is run".[1] Having a dedicated building large enough for everybody involved to meet up is not exactly specified but clearly, for every station, the primary set of kit required to centrally collate, package, schedule and transmit their volunteers' content must be located in the geographical area where their target audiences are based. One might expect that licence holders value having a physical presence in the geographical area within which they operate, a centre of some sort, because it facilitates access to the resources they offer to the community like media skills training. Some station teams aim to part-fund their activities through setting up a charity shop or café as well as providing some-where people can meet. It is also useful from the public awareness point of view for a station to be visible in a locality, so that potential listeners, volunteers and contributors of content, as well as advertisers, notice it and use it.

Describing and positioning a station through branding and publicity materials as "local" rather than "community" can help establish local credibility and raison d'être. This tactic is also driven by the desire to distance the organization from any amateurish, grassroots or even ac-tivist connotations and to convey professionalism which can help in the sale of airtime to bring in much-needed income. This was certainly the case for Radio Verulam in St Albans. The attitude of the station's di-rectors was that they were the only radio broadcasting service in and for their district since the area's mainstream stations were at best providing a regional service. Their approach to raising funds was focussed on the selling of airtime and programme sponsorship, so broadcast output sounded commercialized. However, they argued that they were deli-vering entertainment and information tailored around what residents and locally invested organizations wanted and needed. This resonates with government thinking behind the eventual introduction of the third tier community-led radio sector; it is a way of ensuring independently funded, not-for-profit local broadcasting provision whilst satisfying the grassroots fuelled demand for access radio.

The example of the short-lived internet station in Harpenden, is a good reminder that one of the ingredients for a radio station to survive and thrive is the concerted effort spent on nurturing a sense of com-munity amongst its practitioners. The team behind the online station had aspirations to apply for an Ofcom licence, but with no place for its volunteers to gather in person and no encouragement to mix on virtual platforms, there was very little opportunity for the group to bond and the participating contributors as well as the audience were too easily neglected (Browne, 2012). Without teamwork and engagement, the ar-rangements of an organization will not feature the interrelations and connections that need to be formed by its members in order for arrays of activities to be performed, for protocols and conventions to be estab-lished and implemented, in pursuit of the collectively embraced purpose.

As my research has indicated, management protocols differed from station to station, as did the physical infrastructural arrangements. Although the stations were kitted out with broadly similar technolo-gies, teams had developed their own routines for gathering contribu-tions from volunteers for the broadcast schedules, websites and across their social media. The Eye appeared to run along family lines, with the hospitable, supportive, long-suffering parents at the top of the tree. The close-knit community spirit was cemented though online engagement and occasional get togethers, including annual festive dinners and award ceremonies. There was a high degree of mutual trust amongst the team. One aspect which left the station vulnerable however, was that there did not appear to be a formal, ongoing recruitment and training programme: new recruits were serendipitously discovered when they contacted the station to publicize an event, were interviewed on-air or encountered socially. This made it hard to provide cover for certain shows, especially those which demanded a higher degree of competence and confidence like the sports show. How fair was it that Christine and Patrick routinely stepped in, literally through their kitchen door to present for hours at a time, filling gaps in the schedule?

The radio stations which were run along much more hierarchical lines such as Vibe and Verulam sounded slick with well-produced shows and a good supply of talent. Turnover in relation to the producers, presenters and other volunteers involved in operations did occur but not often enough to disrupt. I detected a pattern at Vibe that indicated even after volunteers had finished training they stayed on, wanting to remain involved, which says something for the value they attached to the relationships they had formed there and their sense of belonging and commitment to the station and to its purpose. Radio LaB's station coordinator was accustomed to losing volunteers frequently by virtue of it being a student-led station and looked forward to a new intake each year. This was a situation that they routinely worked around each summer, but it did leave the station particularly vulnerable under the unexpected circumstances brought about by the COVID-19 pandemic, when so many students departed sooner than expected and the local pool of townsfolk talent also dried up. The crisis situation highlighted how the loss of the physical station hub impacted upon the feeling of connection experienced by the people who usually contributed shows and features. The presenters were prevented from using the equipment in the studio hub where they felt more confident in their ability and were usually able to get together in their teams to inspire and boost each other's confidence. This contributed to a diminution of their productive efforts.

The online spaces of community radio

Every community radio station in the UK has its own website or equivalent online presence, conveying material including: history and other official information such as contact pages, their licence agreement or key commitments statement; current programme schedule; profiles of the presenters, often with portraits of them in action; galleries of photographs showing outside broadcast and other promotional activities out and about in the local area; what's on listings, event diaries and blogs. These are useful resources not only for audiences but for the station practitioners when they seek out content ideas and try to build a following for their shows. In addition, online hubs provide links to stream or listen live using the Community Media Association's (CMA) Canstream, the RadioPlayer app or equivalent, as well as or alternatively providing a click through to a standalone service such as TuneIn. Once aired, entire shows are available online in regularly updated "listen again" sections or edited into more compact versions of presenter interviews with guests and contributors and uploaded as more enduring podcasts. Most sites carry hyperlinks to podcast services, Twitter accounts and other social media platforms such as Facebook, Instagram, blog pages and music platforms.

In my own practice of creating features for the online local radio station in Harpenden, I enhanced the value of the audio content being streamed with written text and photographs posted alongside in blogs and social media platforms. I knew that online interaction would be important for attracting listeners to the audio. It would also potentially raise awareness of the station's existence as well as the organizations featured in each of my episodes, perhaps encouraging listening to other content in the station's schedule. My research revealed that visual content was widely used amongst practitioners and did not detract from the value of the audio offering, rather it added to the listener experience and was a powerful publicity tool and public relations tactic. Being visible and active online makes a station appear more approachable to listeners, enhances the listening experience and even facilitates face-to-face encounters in the studios and at public events.

The listenership, those people imagined to be listening in the minds of presenters, are not only addressed in a very personal, one-to-one manner in the virtual spaces of radio programmes. Now listeners can be visualized too, if they engage publicly in the online spaces of a station. Online platforms provide useful analytics from activity for measuring engagement with the content. For instance, Terry at Radio LaB reported that their Facebook page had 3,000 followers as did the Twitter account. One Vibe producer recounted how they exploited social media to create a buzz around their weekly local music show and encouraged listeners to make an appointment to listen. The record was 800 individual listens on different devices at one moment in time.

Digital technologies and producing radio content

From studio observations and networking over the last few years, I have noticed how technological innovations have been incorporated into familiar looking spaces and the delicate interplay of practices and arrangements has shifted and evolved. Radio practitioners have adapted to using new tools for making radio, but conventions are perpetuated, such as attention paid to the acoustic environment of studios; they are still soundproofed and furnished in similar ways to the pre-digital age. We use the same lexicon in our practice, for instance, we might still say the recorded material is "in the can", we "mark", "cut" and "paste" it during the editing process and even "broadcast" it as "radio" even though it is being simulcast or posted online. Digital technologies have been exploited by those working in the radio industry in ways which have both contributed and responded to cultural shifts in listening habits. Listeners are accustomed to radio being conversational good company, up to date and informational, musically and theatrically entertaining, but have come to appreciate and expect the additional visual content that complements and supplements their overall enjoyment. They engage with a station's range of outputs in real time and afterwards on their own terms. They listen to a local station from afar via the internet on Wi-Fi or mobile data, using apps in a browser or downloaded onto a device, and through pre-coded skills for selecting content on voice-activated, smart speaker systems. I found this versatility of engagement useful for my research as I was able to listen-in to stations remotely and even to particular shows and features at times to suit my own schedule.

Producers and presenters have embraced this reality, too, and strategize how to address it through their delivery style to enhance what they imagine is the listener experience. I heard listeners mentioned and dedications read for people outside stations' respective catchment areas, far from the transmitter and well beyond earshot of an analogue radio set. The presenters in my research regularly reminded their listeners of the various ways they could hear the station and their favourite shows, and there were frequent promotional trails inviting listeners to tune in and join in on traditional radios, online, smartphones and smart speakers. When conventions in an industry shift significantly, as they did in broadcasting around the turn of this century, these instigate repercussions which are initially unsettling and cause concern. In local BBC (British Broadcasting Corporation) stations for instance, reporters were increasingly expected to train in bi-media reporting and sent out into the field with not only audio recording equipment but a camera or video camera (Cottle and Ashton, 1999). As well as scripting and producing radio reports, they were expected to supply articles, photographs and video reports for their station's website. Apart from the obvious threat to jobs, with fewer people covering more tasks, the approach made sense because internet platforms became so significant in the integrated provision of local content. In the commercial sector too, this converged media-gathering approach has facilitated more cost-effective coverage of localities but with greatly reduced staff in-situ. The larger corporations optimize profitability through extending their regional networks across the country, merely paying lip service to local affairs from centralized hubs.

Seeing the production of content as a social site reveals similarities between community radio and mainstream contexts. I observed volunteers taking on numerous roles such as presenter, producer, reporter, marketing, sales: all recognizable positions elsewhere in the industry. They were performing similar tasks, using the same equipment and sets of skills as professionals use. The difference is that whilst it may bring a little glory for the practitioner in the community at large, this work in the third tier is predominantly voluntary. Even where staff were paid, they put in extra hours. For the community sector then, media convergences have not threatened the workforce because the majority of presenters and producers are not paid anyway. In some cases, they even contribute money to the running costs of a station through membership fees.

Assuming a community radio organization can afford to purchase new equipment, software programs and licences, the challenge is how to attract enough volunteers, train them up on the technologies and keep them motivated to help produce output. It is also beneficial for a station's members to be active on social media. To maximize the impact of a station's operations in the name of social gain, exposure is important, so self-promotion is a necessity. The culture of liking, following and sharing generates publicity. As adept as one can be at dual screening, there are limits to the extent a radio presenter can multi-task. In the community sector, it is even more important to work in teams and for presenters to have a studio assistant or producer to take responsibility for tweeting about, quoting and posting photographs of guests and contributors who are visiting the station. From a practical point of view too, during a live show or a tightly timed studio session, presenters require help to deal with these visitors.

The listening-in research I conducted prior to the pandemic demonstrated that most of the community radio shows were transmitted live, although some were routinely pre-recorded for later broadcast out of convenience. When presenters pre-recorded a programme, even at home, they generally aimed to do so under live and timed conditions, delivering their material in a manner as if they were communicating live with a co-present audience. This proved to be more efficient from a "time-it-takes" perspective; having spent hours preparing a show, more confident volunteers would not allow themselves additional time to listen back or redo it. Experience in radio presentation brings with it the reassurance that perfection in speech delivery on-air, as in real conversation, is rarely achieved and that is precisely what makes radio talk sound personable and feel natural (Goffman, 1981; Scannell, 1991).

Providing local coverage

In my exploration of how digital technologies were implicated in practitioner routines, I focussed on what I perceived to be the distinctive teleoaffective structure of the community sector. By this I mean, the shared sense of purpose and commitment that motivates someone to cover issues and topics which matter to audiences in a specific geographical locality with the ultimate aim of delivering social gain. The specific tactics and objectives varied from person to person and station to station, but they all belonged to the same practice of producing local community-oriented content. As discussed in earlier chapters, locally based stations are well-placed to provide localized coverage of current affairs and events. The activities involved in media production practice within the community sector overlap with those of mainstream operators of local services and other entities such as hyperlocal news websites. Another instance where independent media production activities interweave with community radio is citizen journalism (Atton, 2008). However, I see a distinction between what is understood as grassroots reporting and what community stations deliver through offering to train and provide airtime, empowering individuals to report on news events where and when they unfold, using mobile and digital technology.

A community broadcasting licence carries a responsibility to ensure that whilst, in theory, anyone anywhere can tell their own story or express their views on someone else's, care must be taken to avoid negative consequences. Any reporting of stories deemed as news should be measured against certain accepted standards, limited by the framework of the Broadcasting Code and UK libel laws. News reporters should be appropriately trained, and their performances supervised. Support, guidance and funding for community broadcasters in the provision of actual news coverage has been patchy and organic. In some cases, The Memorandum of Understanding arrangement with the BBC's English Regions division provides mentoring, training and opportunities for mutual exchanges of content, but not all community stations have been able to build the links. It worked for Somer Valley FM (SVFM) for instance, because Dom already had BBC connections. The BBC's Local Democracy Reporting service, as part of its renewed Charter, involves funding the provision of trained journalists to local media companies, but this policy-driven attempt to solve the issue of dwindling local news coverage has prioritized online and newspaper publishers. There is widespread critical monitoring of mainstream news providers by "publics" on social media, and the BBC often comes under fire. Yet at the same time, the circulation of distorted journalism and fake news on those same platforms is a matter for concern. UK communications regulator, Ofcom, and educational bodies tackle media literacy with this in mind, and as this counts as social gain, it is deemed something that the community sector can help deliver. The problem here though is that these small, under-funded stations often lack a newsroom in which volunteers and members of the community could be instructed in how to look for the origins of a story, weigh up different perspectives and seek out the truth or at least a balanced viewpoint.

Consequently, some practitioners I consulted did not think their station delivered "news" in the hard news sense – time-sensitive, hard-hitting, political – and they felt they would not be able to respond to a dramatic event in the same way a mainstream station might. Nevertheless, upon reflection they did agree that they were in a good position to access and circulate information that needed disseminating. In this sense then, other qualifying indicators of newsworthiness came into play: proximity; human interest; relatability; rarity; concerning conflict or celebrity. Presenters' conversations, appearances and activities on-air and online created opportunities and inspiration for stories to develop organically. People in the news could contribute their side or discuss how they were affected in more detail than was conveyed in print. Such information was imparted in magazine-style shows, through interviews and discussions on local affairs, newspaper reviews and commentary, phone-ins, reportage on particular topics, and even live artist performances to publicize forthcoming events.

Presenters were not routinely imparting sensational information, but more "general" items which lacked immediacy: their output lay somewhere between soft and hard news (Lehman-Wilzig and Seletzky, 2010, p. 51), resonating on a more "feminine" register (ibid., p. 39).

The type of content and style of delivery conformed broadly to the "human interest" infotainment tactics ascribed to the new national independent broadcasters from the 1990s (Starkey and Crisell, 2009, p. 19). This has been dubbed "newszak" (Franklin, 1997), and synonymized with "tabloidization" (Reinemann et al., 2011, p. 234). However, I agree with An Nguyen and eschew the normative, elitist trivializing of this softer form of journalism because "for ordinary citizens, soft news is an important part of daily life" (Nguyen, 2012, p. 707), and community radio excels at conveying it.

That said, my research demonstrated that station managers did have confidence in the ability of at least a minority of their volunteers who were sufficiently equipped and experienced to respond to a breaking news situation or conduct an investigation. I remind you here of the phenomenon of "in-betweeners" (Ahva, 2017, p. 143): media professionals and freelance journalists who volunteer in the community sector. These reporters would be trusted to venture out and produce content to circulate on-air and online. There were also opportunities for station presenters to interview local newspaper reporters, politicians or spokespersons about arising crises or potential scandals but usually the ideal of holding authority to account and upholding local democracy took a back seat in relation to more innocuous information provision. In any case, it might be argued that local stations have too much at stake in their localities to rock the boat with too much critical reporting on local current affairs. Building sympathetic networks with local supporters and funders is paramount for ensuring the longevity of a station. They were reliant on good relations, cultivating positive relationships, focussing on consensus building and non-confrontational day-to-day programming. I found that community radio teams were motivated to promote what was good, where was good and who was good around their area.

My research has revealed multiple ways in which digital technologies enable practitioners to perform their content production roles effectively and efficiently. In recognition of one of the eternal challenges of speaking into a microphone, I have categorized them as a list of terms all beginning with the sibilant letter "s".

Sourcing

Online sources are nearly always used in programme planning these days. Studio computers are provided for volunteers to search for content from trusted news and information websites, but they are also at liberty to take smartphones and other personal devices into live studios. So, whereas traditionally, practitioners would communicate with contributors and listeners by letter or telephone they can now keep in touch and abreast via email, direct messaging on social media or by text without even leaving their studio console. The organized volunteer follows themed hashtags and feeds of selected people, organizations and topics which they think their audience will be interested in. Correspondence with listeners yields ideas for news items, suggestions of new artists to feature, or events that the station could publicize or cover. Not only are mobile phones used in setting up or conducting interviews, but they have made on-location reporting easier and cheaper. There is no longer a need to book an expensive temporary landline, buy or rent a radio car with an aerial for linking back to the station, or for the reporter to find a conveniently located office or public telephone in order to contact the studio. Smartphone apps such as Luci Live, enable the broadcasting of entire live shows from outside the studios. An increasingly popular means of accessing content has been through conducting interviews via online conferencing platforms and browser based audio feeds: a range of software suppliers offer free basic accounts which meet professional broadcast quality standards such as Zoom and Cleanfeed.

Sifting

An infinite number of webpages can be searched, bookmarked and refreshed when required. A potential disadvantage is the temptation to surf too many sites, potentially wasting time, finding too much information, or becoming distracted when fact-checking. Developing a disciplined approach to internet searches is a prerequisite to the efficient exploitation of that resource. Faced with a glut of material, it is important to learn how to discern what has value and is accurate. Whilst exploring the internet might yield unexpected, serendipitous or random information that would add value to a show's content, it is advisable to have a list of favourite or trusted websites and pages. Self-discipline for time-management reasons is important, as is disciplining a station's volunteers to be consistent with a streamlined approach that ensures uniformity in the reliable delivery of useful, trustworthy information. For example, Verulam maintained group resources in the cloud for the presenters, such as a template for traffic and travel with the recommended links to prime data providers.

Serving

Presenters are routinely prompted by the system or their own show timetable to refer to listings for local happenings like school fairs, sports fixtures, exhibitions, talks and fundraisers. They also find that having such material available can be useful for filling the conversational gap in case of a timing miscalculation or other contingency. Stations' own intranets or private groups and pages on social media platforms carry a wealth of information supplied by colleagues or curated by station management that can be used, and their websites carry event diaries with details provided by the public. This service is pivotal in ensuring that local clubs, businesses, organizations, charities and community groups benefit from associating with community radio; promotional exposure via the station's social media as well as broadcast output helps keep them ticking over by staying in the public mind's eye and in word of mouth circulation.

Saving

My evidence suggests that these non-professional yet competent practitioners benefit greatly from the advantages of digitally enabled mobility, spatial freedom and time shifting. Most of my respondents described using their own smartphones to record interviews and actuality out on location. This means they do not have to invest in specialist equipment like digital recorders. Either way, saving audio is easily done and just as easily transferred to other devices to work on later. There is widespread use of portable tablets and laptops as well as home desktop computers for production work: recording and editing for upload into cloud-based accounts. Other data such as documents, notes on stories, ideas for features, interview and quiz questions can be conveniently saved in the same manner. For instance, Verulam's Sunday lunchtime presenter collected local trivia, lists of competitions questions and quiz titles on his smartphone, enough to last him the entire year and beyond, all about famous local people, well-known buildings and interesting facts.

Storing

Digital innovations spelled the end to the "evanescent-by-default" nature of broadcast radio's content. Archiving systems have made it possible to store vast amounts of audio material, lengthening the shelf life of a station's products and creating additional opportunities for boosting audience consumption and engagement. In terms of handling all this content and data, putting systems in place is important. Developing procedures for filing details and contacts so that they will be retrievable when needed is the sensible approach, particularly when time is of the essence. Of course, this creates a dependency on the equipment functioning correctly. When a computer crashes, the phone signal drops, batteries run out or there is no space remaining on the memory card, you need the contingency back-ups and hard copies of information, even handwritten. The example of Verulam's sports show illustrates how important show notes are, reinforcing the enduring value of "old" or legacy media to the practice.

Shaping

I apply this term to those processes whereby material is prepared for broadcast or posting online. Audio editing is undertaken at community stations but not by all practitioners. As my research has shown, some prefer to do everything live. They script and plan as best they can in advance and "wing it" for best results. User friendly, open source software such as Audacity is freely available, or stations can get deals on proprietary program licenses. In my own practice, I spent many happy hours carefully editing and layering tracks, crafting my ten features. Yet, I encountered volunteers who were reluctant or felt unable to learn how to edit. Training can be offered by station management or colleagues and there are online tutorials on platforms such as YouTube. At the end of the day, it depends on how much time volunteers are prepared to spend on station chores and what sort of access they have to the station in order to use the equipment. As findings in the following section will illustrate, it also depends on whether volunteers are prepared or able to invest their own money in digital equipment to use at home.

Sharing

My use of the term "sharing" covers the transmission of a station's output but also how producers submit the content they have produced to their station to be broadcast. If they are broadcasting live, which is normally what most volunteers do, then their show is transmitted directly to the listeners. But audio is simultaneously streamed and recorded: both for monitoring purposes and to provide the listen again facility. If the practitioners are recording as-live from the studio, they record into the system, via number-coded carts. If they are voice-tracking from a studio or from home using software and online sharing services like WeTransfer and Dropbox, they record their audio links to be uploaded automatically into the playlist between music and other fixtures. Sharing in relation to radio content is also connected to the online realm where output is remediated as shareable clips and podcasts.

Screening

Linked to the above are the screens used to view websites and social media platforms where all manner of audio-visual and visual content generated through station activities is made available: articles and blogs, photographs and videos of guest interviews and performances, promotional and fundraising stunts. The visual presence of these items brings useful marketing and promotional benefits for a station, its presenters and the many local organizations, events, schemes and projects that are featured.

Surveying

By sharing, storing and screening content online, it is possible to survey who is engaging with the station, to monitor listener and user reactions. Audience members become visible on social media platforms such as Facebook, Twitter and Instagram: at least those individuals prepared to reveal themselves rather than lurk or remain anonymous. Reactions to a station's output provide some idea of how many listeners are interested, which is useful for pitching to potential advertisers to sell airtime and sponsorship opportunities. But this exposure works both ways. Interviewees and contributors, politicians and business owners can more easily listen back to themselves and to on-air discussions relating to their activities which potentially renders them more sensitive about how they are portrayed. This means that potentially, station output is more vulnerable to criticism. It has always been the case that stations must record their transmissions and keep those recordings for six weeks in case a complaint to Ofcom needs investigating. Now, there is more chance that a listener who thought they may have heard something untoward can listen again to be sure, and even share the link with friends and colleagues.

Diversity in community radio

Despite its associations with the global field of alternative, grassroots-powered access media, licensed community radio in the UK is heavily regulated. At the time of writing, on the brink of potential digital proliferation with the small-scale multiplex scheme (known as SSDAB), there are around 300 analogue stations in the country. The sector's profile overall is diverse; reading the station names and where they are located indicates the sheer variety of communities served.[2] In this sense, government policy towards providing diversity of programming for the benefit of audiences is paying off. Yet taking a micro perspective to ask who are entrusted to run the stations and whose voices are broadcast reveals scope for improvement, particularly where sociocultural factors and gender are concerned. Where inclusion is affected by aptitude and engrained attitudes towards the use of digital technologies, more needs to be done enabling the disinterested and disenfranchised to overcome any barriers to entry. Community radio ought to be properly "accented" by putting to air authentic voices representing the ethnic and cultural character of the target audience (Moylan, 2018). We must pay attention to where gender intersects with "digital capital" in the usage of technologies from word processing to coding, as Sara De Vuyst does from a feminist point of view in her book on journalism for this *Disruptions* series (De Vuyst, 2020). I cannot claim to present the definitive diagnosis here, but I have captured snapshots from the field symptomatic of the current situation.

Through my own research, I have collected information directly from practitioners in 16% of UK stations, and communicated with more through networking in the sector. As discussed in Chapter Two, there is a small number of bodies with online resources relating to and supporting the sector: the CMA, Radio Regen and newer lobby groups and businesses that have been launched such as The Radio Hub, UK Community Radio Network (UKCRN) for managers, Local Radio Alliance, and advertising consultancy LLR Media (Love Local Radio). The industry trade publication, *Radio Today*, has a community radio section, and naturally, Ofcom, provides general information. For instance, the regulator states: "On average, stations operate with 87 volunteers who together give around 209 hours of their time a week" (Ofcom, 2019). Extrapolating this in line with the reported number of licences listed at the time of writing, n = 299, this would suggest that there were around 26,000 volunteers in community radio (Ofcom, 2020).

Evidence from my online survey conducted during the lockdown yielded useful data and insights on the sector. I find that the number of volunteers is lower, more likely averaging around 45 volunteers per station. Nearly a third of the 44 stations I surveyed (31.8%) had between 21 and 40 people working or volunteering with them, and a quarter had between 41 and 60. Only 9% declared more than 80 volunteers. It was interesting to note that two thirds (65.9%) of the responding stations did not charge a membership subscription. Since the questionnaire was targeted at station managers or directors of equivalent status, I was able to see that over half of those who responded (52.3%) were aged between 51 and 70, and a further 34.1% were aged between 31 and 50. This, added to my personal experience and encounters with station staff, is a strong indicator that middle-aged and retired people are in charge of operations. In terms of gender, 79.5% of respondents to my online survey were male. As for ethnic diversity, my respondents were overwhelmingly white (86.4%). I conducted 12 follow-up interviews which yielded further intelligence as to the demographic breakdowns within specific stations. One London volunteer team was reportedly two thirds women, and four station managers claimed an even 50:50 male to female ratio, the other stations' female contingent was one third or lower. I had selected five female and seven male respondents, based on the extent to which their station programming had changed. I was as much interested in those reporting no change as I was in those who had reported significant changes to their schedules.

Insights from my earlier fieldwork derived from listening-in, surveying programme schedules and websites provided an indication of who was voicing the shows and revealed that, at least in those selected station contexts, gender and cultural diversity was lacking. On the internet station for Harpenden, there were only ever two female presenters. So, in the features I created, I ensured that seven of the 13 contributors were women, ranging in age from 18 to nearly 90. I tried to reflect ethnic diversity in the selection of voices and opinions to be representative despite the town being 93.1% white (based on the 2011 Census); I included voices of Asian and Eastern European residents. At Vibe in Watford, though the volunteer body reflected the target demographic age-wise, their gender and ethnic mix did not. My snapshot study revealed that there were 10 women presenting 14 shows each week, whereas 16 men presented 31. Only three were of Black, Asian and Minority Ethnic (BAME) origin, even though the town was home to over 25,000 BAME residents, accounting for around 28% of the local population. Of the station's three-strong part-time paid staff team, only one was a woman and I did not notice any physically disabled members of the organization.

At Radio LaB in Luton, a town with one of the most ethnically diverse populations in the country, with 45% of the town's residents being BAME, there did appear to be good mix of volunteers.

However, out of 39 weekly shows, 23 men presented 27 of them and there were only nine women. Of the four student managers, two were female and two male. There was no evidence of students with physical disabilities being involved at that time. The Eye was based in a Leicestershire market town which was 97.2% white. Only two of over 60 volunteers were BAME, although the managing director pointed out that the largest ethnic group locally was the Polish community. There were 49 men and 16 women pictured on the gallery of presenters and at the time of my visit in April 2018, of the 59 show slots on the station, only 10 women appeared to present or co-present nine shows, whereas 34 men presented or co-presented 48.

SVFM had around 100 volunteers in 2018. Of 49 shows each week, only five were presented by seven named women, whereas there were 25 named male presenters responsible for 24 shows plus six repeats. The manager and his assistant were both white males, as were all presenters reflecting the very low ethnic diversity in the town: 98.1% white. At Verulam in St Albans where 88% of residents were categorized as white, I observed just four out of 60 volunteers from BAME backgrounds involved with the shows: half what could be considered representative. In addition, although their website featured photographic evidence of multiple female volunteers, there were only 13 women presenting compared to 26 men. Two years after my participant observation there, Clive updated me on their refreshed roster which included eight new female voices.

These figures are disappointing, especially compared to industry employment figures. According to Ofcom's report *Diversity and equal opportunities in radio,* the workforce across all departments including off-air roles comprises 52% women and 48% men (Ofcom 2020). Community radio stations should do better on-air but also do better with those people involved alongside and behind the scenes, producers and studio assistants, trainees and administrators who also contribute to the character of a station and its output, whether in terms of broadcast material, online content, community relations and event organization. Reasons behind the poor gender balance are easy to surmise, such as culturally embedded, preconceived ideas about who makes the best kind of radio presenter or how an individual's availability can be limited by their domestic responsibilities. This is a theme ripe for further analysis but there is not the room here. Ethnic and sociocultural diversity should absolutely be a priority for general interest stations serving mixed populations in geographical areas. Concerted efforts should be made to recruit from minority neighbourhoods and bearing in mind the real costs associated with volunteering, a case can be made for subsidizing their involvement. Stations need to find the balance between pro-actively facilitating increased diversity and maintaining professional standards: building trust amongst their membership in order to maintain community spirit within the organization as well as with the wider communities of listeners beyond their physical and online hubs.

The impact of COVID-19 on the production of local content

The pandemic revealed that not all volunteers are considered equal, since many were excluded from stations' crisis arrangements due to either lack of experience with or access to the available digital resources. Responses to my online questionnaire in June 2020 (see Appendix), showed that management teams had instigated training regimes in the hope that lesser experienced volunteers might commit the time to upskill themselves, and they were trying to find ways of providing equipment to those less well-resourced. When I had conducted an initial sweep through Ofcom's list of licensed stations in April 2020, by clicking through to their online "listen now" feeds, it appeared that the vast majority of stations had been able to maintain broadcast transmissions. They were managing to produce varying amounts of locally produced content during lockdown, presented by personalities familiar to their audiences. Official announcements explaining how programming was affected by lockdown were posted on stations' homepages, along with information on the unfolding crisis and policy developments in their locality and across the country. In May 2020 for instance, Dunoon Community Radio in Argyll and Bute, Scotland, reassured listeners of their continued dedication to providing a local service by publishing this statement on their website:

> To keep you informed of local issues we have changed the format of some programmes with presenters including more local information, many of you will have noticed that the morning [breakfast] Roads, Rail and Rivers show has now almost dedicated itself in informing you to what shops are open and how you can organise home deliveries ... For the past few weeks as presenters entered isolation our IT Department (Archie) was working hard in devising ways and means of presenters broadcasting from their own homes and we now have seven presenters broadcasting with two more shortly to come on line.[3]

Management approaches

I received responses from 44 community station managers to my questionnaire: three of whom had participated in my previous case studies. Analysis demonstrates that the same crisis had differential impacts and necessitated different strategic solutions due to the varying contexts, unique circumstances and differing arrays of available resources and skillsets. I did not hear from The Eye, but I suspect Christine and Patrick continued to manage their broadcast output very well: the main studio was next to their kitchen after all and they already had presenters accustomed to producing and presenting from their own homes. One of the few stations that was not required to shut their doors was SVFM, and this station hub continued to operate with a smaller number of volunteers to maintain an approximately normal service. However, as was the case for other stations engaging in hands-on apprenticeships and training, these activities were compromised, causing potential funding and income issues.

Of all the managers to respond to my survey, almost two thirds of them said their workload had increased during the pandemic. Bearing in mind that the same proportion of them were not paid for their role, and half of them normally worked between 11 and 30 hours per week, this constitutes a highly valuable resource and level of personal commitment. When lockdown had looked likely, management teams deliberated their action plans and decided whether and how their studios could be kept operational and volunteers kept safe. Consideration was taken for the welfare of any members who were shielding or living with vulnerable people, but at the same time every station had their key commitments to deliver. Since face-to-face contact with station teams, volunteers and contributors was restricted, such administrative communications shifted entirely over to phone calls, emails and social media and there was widespread adoption of video conferencing.

Programming priorities steered the stations' crisis-management decisions. The most important consideration for over half the respondents was to achieve a balance between the amount of shows and voices they could get on air and the quality of that output. The chairman at Abbey 104 in Sherborne, Dorset, also employed elsewhere as a full-time engineer, commented: "Quality of sound is not as important as quality of content for local community". And a director/presenter from Vectis Radio on the Isle of Wight said: "The primary aim was to maintain a service and improve on the quality as we progressed. This has been achieved with most presenters finding that inexpensive microphones are good enough, given the generally lower standards of acoustics in their homes".

However, 38.6% were adamant that quality should not be compromised. A director/presenter at Erewash Sound in Ilkeston, Derbyshire explained: "We have a reputation to uphold but we have a loyal, appreciative and understanding listenership, aware of who we are and our place in the community, seen as 'friends' doing a worthy but professional job". Another chair/managing and programme director at Kennet Radio in Newbury, Berkshire pointed out: "We have been able to maintain production values even with some presenters VTing from home with nothing more than a USB mic and a laptop". Some volunteers were self-selecting in stepping back from active presenting during the crisis. Terry at Radio LaB for instance, observed that many volunteers lapsed because:

> ...for so many people involved, their introduction to radio was using our studios. And so, you take them out of the studios, and they lose their confidence. So even if they did record something using a laptop, they would know it wasn't the same... I'm listening with headphones right now and I can't hear myself coming back. And that's off-putting because it's a different environment.

So how were stations able to continue operating when their studios were rendered out of bounds? The respondents were asked a series of questions about their programming routines prior to COVID-19 and how things had changed during lockdown. Just under three quarters of respondents said that under normal conditions, their stations tended to broadcast more live output than pre-recorded content. Not surprisingly, a similar proportion reported that live transmissions had reduced a lot under lockdown as their volunteers adapted to doing their shows remotely. Where the majority of stations had been accustomed to having less than ten remotely produced shows per week, they had been forced into a position where they relied entirely on home-produced content across their schedules. For the fifth of cases who said that there had been no change, this was because either remote production and presentation was already common or they had been able to facilitate limited access to presenters to broadcast from the live studios. Several stations reported that their radio stations were large enough, with two or three studios, to allow for certain essential staff and volunteers to retain access on a rota basis, subject to the areas being deep cleaned and those individuals passing muster health-wise.

For nearly half of the respondents, the shift to remote production had been enabled by the roll-out of voice-tracking (VTing). Use of this technology was already fairly widespread in the commercial sector but according to my findings, there had been only limited take-up in the community sector prior to the COVID-19 outbreak: 68.2% of respondents said that no more than four of their practitioners normally used the approach. However, for a small percentage of cases (11.4%), the usage had reduced a good deal. From comments in follow-up interviews, it was clear that this was because before the pandemic, VTing was conducted in studios which had since been locked down.

As I have indicated, there is such a variety of community radio stations across the country operating within unique sets of circumstances, that there is no one-size-fits-all model for how each set-up functions. The extent to which station teams felt prepared in terms of technology, skilled volunteers and other resources varied significantly. Overall, one group of respondents, accounting for almost a third of the sample, said they "just about had adequate access to some basic resources". An equal proportion expressed that they "were fairly well-equipped". There were stations less well prepared. I learned that Radio Tyneside in Newcastle upon Tyne "had nothing in place", and Keith Community Radio (KCR FM) based in Moray, Scotland, told me: "Few of our presenters are technically minded, several don't use computers/tablets/smart phones at all". Sometimes though, solutions could be found. The station manager at Abbey 104 stated: "A lot of [the] older generation of presenters were taught new skills and bought their own equipment". What those who felt they were "excellently resourced" had in common was software and the availability of decent quality devices: the director at recently launched Black Cat Radio for St Neots in Cambridgeshire reported that they had already "purchased a new playout system that allowed every presenter to be live or voice track (VT) from home".

Programme schedules

My survey found that the most important factor for determining which volunteers could continue broadcasting was possession of the relevant technical know-how, closely followed by internet access. So, I was interested in what impact those decisions had on whether stations had been able to keep to their usual programme rosters. Prior to lockdown, over two thirds of responding stations had between 28 and 45 shows on their weekly schedules. When asked how much this had changed under lockdown, over a fifth said they had struggled to maintain normal output. Of the shows still being aired, I wanted to know if they sounded the same. Over a third of the survey respondents, like Terry at Radio LaB, said that most of what they were broadcasting, over 75% of their lockdown content, sounded the same as usual, whilst one quarter of respondents reported that their station sound remained unchanged. One respondent, business development manager at Chelmsford Community Radio in Essex, reported that none of their programmes going out on-air sounded the same. This appeared to be related to a significant reduction in live broadcasting during lockdown. Previously, they broadcast several different shows each day on the weekly schedule; half of those were broadcast live with only a handful of presenters routinely producing their work remotely. Under lockdown two new shows were introduced to accommodate more interviews and local information and this was achieved despite the fact that the station barely had the resources and only a handful of volunteers owned equipment for producing radio at home. This situation improved over time as volunteers adapted, bought themselves microphones and lesser experienced volunteers were given guidance to raise the standard of the work they submitted to be uploaded for broadcast.

Chelmsford was not the only station to introduce new programmes and increase the proportion of speech on-air as the pandemic continued. Nearly two thirds reported that new strands of programming had been introduced. Some of these additions could be put down to changes in the availability or involvement of particular presenters and producers, for instance those who suddenly had more time on their hands to help out because they had been placed on furlough by their employers. There were also cases where stations were approached by DJs offering to contribute music shows. Data from my research indicated that community stations normally rely heavily on music shows for their output. Over half of the respondents estimated that prior to the pandemic they broadcast between 10% and 25% speech content, and almost a third said they routinely produced 25% to 50%. Although over half of the stations surveyed were maintaining their usual speech to music balance, a quarter of station teams had managed to increase their speech content a little, compared with a fifth who had seen a reduction.

Overall, the ability of the station teams to continue broadcasting was impressive and it was clear from the responses to my survey and during the interviews that the extra hours and additional responsibilities weighing upon management and the higher skilled and better equipped volunteers were taking their toll. As Verulam's programme controller commented: "We've noticed that the workload on a few people has dramatically increased to the point of some serious stress issues and frustrations and anger because this is huge dumping on a core of people". Efforts were made to raise public awareness and present proof to Ofcom and other stakeholders of the hard work these community volunteers were putting in. One initiative that generated a good deal of attention was a call to collective action to celebrate their achievements on social media called #radiofromhome day on the 1st of May. Devised by the UKCRN, the campaign kicked off with multiple stations taking part playing the same Beatles track, "All you need is love", at 9:15 am and involved presenters posting photographs of themselves broadcasting from their homes.

Community action stations

Practitioners and administrators within the community sector responded remarkably well to the crisis circumstances. Social distancing and the lockdown scenario spurred people to experiment and implement new ways of doing things. Procedures and processes that volunteers had perhaps been reluctant to adopt or had not taken seriously before, became imperative if they wanted to continue performing their role in the new set of arrangements. Station teams devised ways of reporting on the rapidly and sometimes confusing situation surrounding COVID-19 as it unfolded, especially in cases where the national advice was different or inappropriate for local conditions. Existing routines of communicating with contributors by telephone, text, email and social media continued, but where conducting and recording interviews over the phone or online had once been the exception for some volunteers, it became the norm for everyone. Despite the detached experience of doing everything remotely, station volunteers became acutely aware of the power that lay in their hands for keeping the local community informed, up to date and connected; they realized the true value of their station for contributing to the welfare of many of their listeners.

Station teams were able to act in a public service role by providing coverage of issues specific to their localities, conveying often vital information, notifications about the availability of resources and contact details of charities and other organizations that were offering support and assistance to residents. Cooperating with existing local partners and building new relationships, they delivered enhanced coverage of local health and welfare provision as well as updates from local councils, schools, police and emergency services, trading and charitable organizations. There were instances where stations had started broadcasting local church services and extended airtime for local *Talking Newspapers*. Operators were able to bail out organizers of music festivals which had to be cancelled, by replacing scheduled programming with concerts: broadcasting the events on-air and streaming online. Some stations created their own health and well-being features, others also broadcast government messages and special audio packages by independent producers.

Formal procedures for local news provision and the more informal softer journalistic coverage of local current affairs increased and improved out of necessity. Prior to the lockdown, 59.1% of respondents operated their own local news service, providing content through on-air bulletins and magazine shows and online via social media and station websites. Most (84.6%) said they had been able to maintain this service, if not increase it. Of the stations who previously did not have their own news service, 38.9% of respondents said that they had since started new features, circulating community news on COVID-19-related projects and initiatives.

Whether these displays of apparent resilience and organizational agility will prove sustainable over time is yet to be seen. How long can volunteer energy levels and enthusiasm last and more importantly, where will the money come from to pay the bills? Though some stations did not usually charge their volunteer members a mandatory annual subscription to belong, many received regular donations and voluntary contributions from their active practitioners. These funds were in danger of drying up in the same way that advertising and sponsorship income from local businesses had already reduced dramatically. There were some stations, such as KCR FM, which benefited from the government's Small Business grant. Even so, the station's chair/technical director told me they were reconsidering plans they had made for expansion. With the amount of homeworking their volunteers were becoming accustomed to, would there ever be a need for a second studio? Their elderly or disabled volunteers might prefer to work remotely. Indeed, everyone might decide they preferred the new routine and save a fortune on petrol money usually spent driving great distances to the station in its rural location.

When I first interviewed Dom at SVFM in 2018, he was bullish about the sector's success judging by the continual demand for new licences. He had noted that, in about 2009, the average turnover of a community station in the UK was around £74,000, but that by 2016, it had dropped to just above £50,000. He explained:

> The biggest liability to any community station is going to be one of two things. It's either going to be salaries or premises. If you're completely volunteer-oriented it's gonna be premises. Salaries will take you very quickly north of £20,000 and that would be just a part-time.

He mentioned that he knew of stations that were handing back their licences because they could not generate the revenue which was a matter of concern. "The answer is", he said, "it needs to resource itself better". What hope is there then for the sector post-pandemic?

Community radio in the UK does seem to have come into its own during the COVID-19 crisis. Its profile has increased through trending on social media and appearing occasionally in the mainstream press. But this is paradoxical since most stations have faced disastrous losses of income. So much so, that Ofcom stepped in to bring forward the annual distribution of monetary awards as considered by the independent Community Radio Fund Panel. The first round in May granted 81 requests amounting to £333,152. In August, the panel met again and were able to pay out to 31 of 77 applicants: grants totalled £73,658 ranging from £500 to £5,088, with an average of £2,376.[4] Priority was given to stations that could prove they were in most need of equipment to enable home broadcasting and to support those stations that would otherwise cease broadcasting. Ofcom also announced a temporary scheme for RSLs "designed specifically to share information, news and updates about the COVID-19 pandemic with their community".[5]

Conclusion

This chapter has presented multiple accounts of how local content is produced in UK community radio stations, contextualizing insights from fieldwork alongside evidence from desk research and further socially distanced but no-less in-depth research into the experiences and attitudes of practitioners and managers. I have presented data that indicate there is still progress to be made across the sector when it comes to recruiting bodies of volunteers who are representative of the diversity in their localities but are also gender balanced and inclusive of lesser abled and disadvantaged people. I have discussed the value to a radio station of having a physical studio building but also the sociability that can be created and nurtured on virtual and online spaces, connecting people through a shared sense of belonging to and vested interests in a particular place. I recognize that such place-based social networks associated with community radio audiences are also outward-looking and the members concerned with global affairs too. Vital to all of this is the range of digital media and communication technologies that enable practitioners to carry out their roles in the running of community stations and in the on-going production of programme content and features.

I have argued that this coverage is achieved through both deliberate news-gathering strategies and more organic processes that simply emerge out of presenters always needing new and interesting material to talk about that they feel will resonate with their local listeners. I have applied the term soft journalism to denote how updating audiences on local happenings is achieved and delivered on community stations, where the information is not always conveyed through rolling news updates or up-to-the-minute, on-the-spot reports but through in-show conversations. I have touched on how stations position themselves as "local radio" rather than as something less professional and more grassroots, potentially eschewing the utopian model of community media. With income generation for these non-profit organizations being such a priority for funding their activities and updating studio and broadcast equipment, what provision are they also making for delivering on the community radio ethos of social gain?

The pandemic has cast a fresh light on these questions. I described how the enforced lockdown of organizations and institutions across the country, impacted practice-arrangements in a range of volunteer-dependent stations. In most cases, production and broadcast studios were closed leading to a shift of social interaction and production to online spaces conducted from people's homes. This was achieved because of the affordances of digital technology. In the context of radio production, these are the same technologies that enable internet-only webcasting radio stations to operate and for independent podcasters to produce and distribute content. Overnight, community stations transformed into set-ups that resembled the hubless online station of my practice-based research: the station with no physical headquarters or social centre.

These practice-arrangements are in some ways a throw-back to a past model of how to get a radio station established. In other ways they relate to the many internet-only stations, and perhaps are also a sign of things to come. The crisis response to the material re-arranging of the production line feeding every station's programme schedule resulted in radical changes to individual practitioner routines; some people had to work more intensively and for longer, whilst others found themselves redundant. The station teams settled into a new way of working and found they could feed the system just as well by working remotely. The community spirit prevailed, and means were found to make up for the fact that volunteers and contributors could not meet in person. Yet there have been unfair consequences, too, in terms of accessibility for certain groups. Those finding themselves constrained for space or quietness in their domestic environments were at a disadvantage and the digital divide was a barrier to those less well-versed or equipped.

As in many industries, the question now is whether the normal practice-arrangements from before the pandemic will be resumed when we emerge from the crisis. What does the fact that stations seem to function without their members routinely, and regularly, convening physically in a central hub, mean for the future of the sector? In the following and concluding chapter I consider the pros and cons of digital technologies in the context of the production of local content for community radio stations. Will stresses, strains and disadvantages arise with remote production and presentation that drive operators to decide on a full-scale return to station-based production? Assuming these services can be sustained through the pandemic, what will station teams need to do in terms of making provision for buildings, studios and communal meeting spaces? Station operators work tirelessly to generate sufficient funds to keep running; if it is feasible to sustain a broadcasting service with minimum physical infrastructure, what impels them to maintain that outmoded model? There are implications of this for academic interpretations of radio per se, but I consider what it means for the practice of local community radio broadcasting when being part of the community is so fundamental to its existence.

Notes

1 https://www.ofcom.org.uk/manage-your-licence/radio-broadcast-licensing/community-radio (accessed 07.09.20.).
2 https://www.commedia.org.uk/map/ (accessed 09.10.20.).
3 https://dunooncommunityradio.org/ (accessed 29.05.20.).
4 https://www.ofcom.org.uk/tv-radio-and-on-demand/information-for-industry/radio-broadcasters/community-radio-fund/award-of-grants-2020-21-round-2 (accessed 16.12.20)
5 https://www.ofcom.org.uk/manage-your-licence/radio-broadcast-licensing/apply-for-a-radio-broadcast-licence/temporary-srsl (accessed 29.08.20.).

References

Ahva, L., 2017. How is participation practiced by "in-betweeners" of journalism?. *J. Pract. 11* (2–3), 142–159. 10.1080/17512786.2016.1209084.

Atton, C., 2008. Alternative and citizen journalism. In: Wahl-Jorgensen, K., Hanitzsch, T. (eds), *The Handbook of Journalism Studies*. Routledge, New York; London, 265–278.

Browne, D.R., 2012. What is "community" in community radio? A consideration of the meaning, nature and importance of a concept. In: Gordon, J. (ed.), *Community Radio in the 21st Century*. Peter Lang, Bern, Switzerland, 153–173.

Coleman, J.F., 2020. *UK community radio production responses to COVID-19*. Available from: http://bura.brunel.ac.uk/handle/2438/21156.

Cottle, S., Ashton, M., 1999. From BBC newsroom to BBC newscentre: on changing technology and journalist practices. *Convergence 5* (3), 22–43. 10.1177/135485659900500304.

De Vuyst, S. 2020 *Hacking Gender and Technology in Journalism*. Routledge, Abingdon, Oxon; New York. Available from: https://books.google.co.uk/books?id=BWXMDwAAQBAJ.

Franklin, B., 1997. *Newszak and News Media*. Arnold, London . Available from: https://books.google.co.uk/books?id=OLppQgAACAAJ.

Goffman, E., 1981. *Forms of Talk*. Blackwell, Oxford.

Hemmingway, E., 2008. *Into the Newsroom: Exploring the Digital Production of Regional Television News*. Routledge, London.

Lehman-Wilzig, S.N., Seletzky, M., 2010. Hard news, soft news, "general" news: the necessity and utility of an intermediate classification. *Journalism* 11 (1), 37–56. 10.1177/1464884909350642.

Moylan, K., 2018. Accented radio: articulations of British Caribbean experience and identity in UK community radio. *Glob. Media Commun.* 14 (3), 283–299. 10.1177/1742766518780180.

Moylan, K., 2019. *The Cultural Work of Community Radio*. Rowman & Littlefield International, London; New York. Available from: https://books.google.co.uk/books?id=6OCGDwAAQBAJ.

Nguyen, A., 2012. The effect of soft news on public attachment to the news. *J. Stud.* 13 (5–6), 706–717. 10.1080/1461670X.2012.664318.

Ofcom, 2019. *Community radio*, Ofcom. Available from: https://www.ofcom.org.uk/manage-your-licence/radio-broadcast-licensing/community-radio (accessed 08.09.20.).

Ofcom, 2020. *Ofcom | Community Radio Stations*, Ofcom. Available from: http://static.ofcom.org.uk/static/radiolicensing/html/radio-stations/community/community-main.htm

Ofcom, 2020. *Diversity and equal opportunities in television and radio 2019/20. Report on the UK-based broadcasting industry*. Ofcom. Available from: https://www.ofcom.org.uk/__data/assets/pdf_file/0022/207229/2019-20-report-diversity-equal-opportunities-tv-and-radio.pdf. (accessed 15.12.20.).

Reinemann, C., *et al.*, 2011. Hard and soft news: a review of concepts, operationalizations and key findings. *Journalism* 13 (2), 221–239. 10.1177/1464884911427803.

Scannell, P. (ed.), 1991. *Broadcast Talk*. SAGE Publications, London; New Delhi.

Schatzki, T.R., 2002. *The Site of the Social: A Philosophical Account of the Constitution of Social Life and Change*. Pennsylvania State University Press, University Park, PA.

Starkey, G., Crisell, A., 2009. *Radio Journalism*. SAGE Publications, London.

5 Keeping radio local in the digital age

Introduction

This concluding chapter reflects on the contribution of my research to understandings of audio production and creating radio content for local audiences. Content can take the form of topical conversation, current affairs features, news bulletins and a range of information and entertainments shared in broadcasts across the programme schedules, and related multimedia outputs shared online and via social media. By bringing together multiple perspectives, I have explored how digital technologies are used in sourcing programme material derived from and deemed to be of interest to geographically demarcated target audiences. My research into selected social sites of the practice has produced comparable descriptions of how different groups of practitioners routinely performed specific tasks and activities, according to the same shared understandings, conventions and generally accepted common purpose of making local community radio for social gain. I have shown how technological innovations have strengthened the sector's ability to respond and react to not only the shifting media landscape but also to the unanticipated repercussions of the global pandemic. Since there are commonalities in the performance of audio production across the industry, the findings presented and discussed here will resonate beyond the UK licensed community sector.

This book was written during the first year of the COVID-19 pandemic. Throughout 2020, the community radio sector exhibited great resourcefulness, resolve and resilience. Station teams were equipped to adjust their normal operations, to step up and face the strange new circumstances of remote and socially distanced working. The pandemic highlighted the value of radio in a crisis. As well as providing emotional and psychological support, local stations helped individuals, charities and other community groups to develop locally targeted crisis plans and innovate ways of conveying vital information and supplies to those in need. However, the strain on stations' financial arrangements was exacerbated and concerns over their longer-term sustainability were heightened. To highlight the vital role of radio and community media in daily life, I revisit how the field has been theorized over the past century and make an argument for what I believe is the enduring value of local broadcasting. I discuss the business of operating community radio and address ethical concerns that have come to light. I conclude with recommendations for future action and research.

Reflections on "progress" and change

Radio as a communications medium is inextricably linked with developments in technology but when it became institutionalized as an industry for mass broadcasting, the mechanized distribution of entertainment and information swiftly became the subject of critical social analysis. Academics and commentators questioned what benefits it could bring to society when there was also potential for harm if held in the wrong hands. Thus, notions of radio for the public good were incorporated into cultural and political-economy studies, with all the attendant concerns relating to access and ownership, power and empowerment. Since the 1990s, digitization has had significant visual and interactive impacts on radio broadcasting, however, the essence of what counts as communicating through sound endures. The growth in music streaming and podcasting has only served to emphasize the distinctive character of the medium and the practitioner's ability to use this to connect intimately with listeners. The imaginary spaces conjured up through the act of listening are a manifestation of the power of language and other auditory signals. When listeners can imagine other places such as the studio environment described by the presenter or the site of an incident conveyed by a reporter, and if they can put themselves in other people's shoes through the stories they hear, then they are exposed to other ways of living and other ways of thinking. Radio and audio content, when used well, can extend the boundaries of listeners' knowledge, expand their minds and help bridge cultural divides. Hence the passion for the medium persists and belief in its potential for societal healing continues to drive enthusiasts, activists, lobbyists and researchers.

A century on from radio's genesis, understandings of what counts as output have shifted. Firstly, radio remains definable by the well-established convention of using structured programme schedules,

repeated day after day, week after week, providing listeners and practitioners alike with that reassuring sense that life goes on. But now,
audiences expect programmes to be available after the initial transmission, to listen to again or if they missed them first time around:
without having to make their own home recordings. Their choice of
radio station or programme is available on demand wherever and
whenever. Increasingly user-friendly and affordable technologies have
also been adopted by amateurs and people working outside of organizations to produce their own audio content, independent of rigid
timetables and production guidelines. The medium's democratizing
potential inspires new audio producers to claim their own space in the
field as radical disruptors, placing *vox populi* in the hands of the people,
even though the growth of distribution platforms and the lure of
monetization threatens to rein in some of this revolutionary spirit.
Overlaps between podcasts and radio content abound, not only because
so much spoken word broadcast material is made available as podcasts
and vice versa, but arguably the tendency for podcasters to serialize
their content and maintain a rhythm of releasing new material seems
also to provide that reassuring sense of continuity whilst offering the
promise of new auditory experiences.

The second fundamental shift in what listeners have come to expect
from radio is that a station's output will be multimedia and available
on a range of platforms. Stations' identification data are visible,
show titles, presenter names and tracks being played appear on digital
radio receivers, and logos appear on streaming apps. Accompanying
visuals and audio-visual media supplementing the broadcast output
are routinely provided on websites and social media. At the very
minimum a community radio station might maintain a Facebook
page with a link to how listeners can tune in, information on how to
post comments or contact the studio, a photo gallery of presenters
and past events, posts about forthcoming shows and news headlines.
Or a station might have a basic website or blog page with several
sections listing programme schedules, contact details and background
information on the organization. Such visual add-ons are not new to
the medium. Historically, radio stations, personalities, schedules and
shows were publicized in newsletters and magazines. Letters and articles appeared in the press. Books were published to accompany
landmark radio productions, as guides to complement ongoing series.
Listeners could write in, phone or visit the studios. Listening groups
were organized in the early days of the BBC to gauge audience reactions to programmes. Other off-air activities such as public appearances of presenters, roadshows and outside broadcasts, roving

reporters collecting "vox pops" are also long-established tactics for raising awareness of stations and encouraging public engagement.

Thus, digital technologies have not changed what social interrelations are possible between radio stations and their audiences but how dynamically and intensely they are accomplished and where they take place. Nor have innovations and the shift into the audio-visual sphere detracted from the audio experience; they combine to enhance ways of generating engagement with listeners and potential contributors (Bonini et al., 2014; Zoellner and Lax 2017). The practitioner's sense of purpose also remains intact. When they produce and present content that they care about or are interested in, they always have a listener in mind.

The enduring value of local radio

Those same online platforms where content is shared and relationships built are the focal points for sourcing content. The opportunities for audiences to engage with radio stations in virtual spaces lead to interactive behaviours that encourage and enable communities within the target populations to participate in programmes and inspire practitioners with new things to talk about. This ability to participate in the production of media content is associated with freedom of expression. As I mentioned in Chapter One, the ability that audience members have to source, shape and share media content themselves can empower them to contribute to cultural production. As Bird notes though, the public are consuming media all the time, and only a minority will contribute something back that they have produced themselves; she questions whether commenting on social media is really "an act of creativity" (Bird, 2011, p. 512). She points out that citizen journalism can in theory empower the grassroots but this practice is not performed by everyone and the large media organizations often still perform a gatekeeping role (ibid., p. 511), even as they are held to account by activist media commentators for misreporting and bias.

In this infodemic age, when there is a surfeit of information but no one quite trusts its veracity, we navigate a world where people only believe a story when they have seen it published in several different places. Trust in news is declining, but radio remains the most trusted of all media, and social media the least, according to the 2020 European Broadcasting Union report (Speck, 2020). As regards the regulated provision of local news, policy in the UK has partly contributed to, and partly been shaped in reaction to, the retrenchment of local mainstream media. This means that increasingly the responsibility for localized news and media coverage lies in the alternative and community sector. Since it is rare for a community radio station to have its own newsroom with dedicated personnel at the ready to respond to an unforeseen event, how can they achieve this important service?

I found that community radio stations were able to attract journalists as volunteers and had presenters and reporters with experience who could train others to research and present unfolding situations and significant local happenings as news stories. COVID-19 helped to drive home the shared conviction across the sector that what they were doing to create meaningful content for local audiences was worthwhile. Evidence shared in the previous chapter illustrates how this nationwide corps of unpaid practitioners rose to the challenge of keeping their stations on-air and producing content for the schedules by utilizing their existing networks of contacts and creating new relationships with individuals and organizations based in or conducting business in their target market area. Digital technologies enabled practitioners with the requisite skills and arrangements in place to conduct their research for shows remotely as well as present them. Whether delivering the material live or pre-recorded, they retained the sense of liveness. The intimacy and personality of the programmes and presenters remained and contributed to making station outputs entertaining and resonant, as well as informative: creating a sense of community around each station to which listeners were warmly welcomed. The crisis crystallized the meaning of social gain in relation to the vital information and support the community stations were able to contribute to their audiences. My respondents shared an understanding of the societal importance of what they were doing through their radio work and how their roles in providing a local radio service for the targeted communities fitted into the grander scheme of things.

Changes in technology have not redefined what it is to be a radio presenter or what it means to produce local content for a community station, but they have altered the way practitioners negotiate the physical and infrastructural arrangements in how they carry out the tasks and activities involved. Producing content with local audiences in mind reinforces the notion that radio broadcasting is an act of communication. Whether created through music or conversation, entertaining diversions or informative news reports, the interactional and discursive opportunities that are generated by and in relation to radio programmes convey a spirit of sociability. This intangible aspect of broadcasting manifests in the teleoaffective structure experienced by and influencing practitioners' activities in each of the selected social sites. Therefore, volunteers find their radio work meaningful too: for some, it constitutes a significant part of their identity. Working together to feature local content on-air and online, practitioners develop a strong sense of belonging not only to the radio team but to the community their station serves. The sense of rapport, togetherness and bonding over the airing of mutual concerns and interests occurs both in virtual and physical settings. Such ties and connections made between people similarly invested in a common location are invaluable for ensuring ongoing exchanges and reinforcing the bonds within and between communities.

The widescale introduction of digital media technologies across society has not reduced the perceived value of all things local. There is evidence that in this globalized, media-saturated world, "the local" retains cultural value. In fact, there has been something of a turn to the particular and idiosyncratic, especially in the mainstream news media, with journalists seeking out divergences from the norm and individuals with stories to tell, or perspectives to share, which do not necessarily conform to what is trending in public discourse. This type of coverage does not automatically benefit the local or niche interest communities reported upon; one might call it voyeuristic. But local communities and grassroots movements around the world have now been empowered by the same technological advances and can make their own voices heard. The pandemic has served to heighten our awareness of the importance of interpersonal communication, not only on new virtual platforms but in the material settings within which we carry out our daily routines. News coverage during the crisis has also shown that whilst localized material establishes a sense that a station is serving a geographical area, at the same time it sits comfortably alongside more worldly items such as national and international current affairs. My findings prove that local radio continues to play an important role in information provision and the community sector is best placed to do so.

The business of community radio

Community radio is not simply about producing audio for broadcast and disseminating online multimedia content. It is also about active engagement with the audience and stakeholders by building mutually beneficial partnerships, arranging off-air activities and outreach events, running awards and community schemes and maintaining a physical presence in the locality. Running a community radio station requires a business-like approach because of the substantial costs involved and the number of skilled people required to staff it and fulfil those associated roles. Stations achieve this in different ways and in some cases the studios are located in or form part of a meeting space such as community centres, cafés or charity shops. Good relations with other local media as well as with businesses, clubs, charities and other organizations in the catchment area are essential not only for news gathering purposes but for establishing a station's reputation as a community asset. These relationships are particularly important for raising a station's profile and symbolic capital so that it can try to secure funding from sponsorship and through other income-generating schemes.

Best practice examples of maximizing efficiency, building and capitalizing on contacts in the community involve the use of social media platforms. The affordances of technology can be harnessed for relationships to be nurtured within community radio teams and with their stakeholders and supporters. Efficient networking widens the social circles and introduces new partnerships and connections, making it possible not only to source information but contact people who may become regular contributors and have leads for sources of income and volunteer manpower. There is much to be said for the benefit of having a public relations person on the team.

My research suggests that although two thirds or more of station managers are unpaid, in many cases board members and practitioners have impressive careers in broadcasting, media or business administration behind them. The sector is clearly not run by amateurs. There is also a degree of cross-over between sectors in the radio industry in terms of staffing; it is quite common for experienced broadcasters, technicians and freelance broadcasters to be involved in community stations. I encountered media professionals who combined their day jobs with volunteering and helping to train and mentor new recruits. Vibe's online recruitment adverts for new presenters specified applicants should have professional experience. Many of the volunteers I encountered in my research had decades of broadcasting experience, having started out in Hospital Radio as teenagers. They may well have started out wanting to be the next Tony Blackburn or Janice Long, but such hands-on initiation helps practitioners develop an ear for professional-sounding broadcast standards, and instils in them the shared understandings and attitudes relating to listener-focussed broadcasting.

The most pressing issue facing the sector is sustainability, something lobbyists are constantly bringing to the attention of the authorities. It is not only the financial burden which is significant, but the pressures on community radio staff and volunteers in terms of physical and mental stamina. The responsibility for filling 24 hours' worth of shows with appropriate content every day of the week for the foreseeable future weighs heavily on everyone involved, most particularly on the programme controller and management team. Automated playout systems delivering music overnight are invaluable to fall back on, but the conditions of station licences must be adhered to and are monitored by Ofcom. Every dedicated practitioner is driven by their conscience and personal commitment to their listeners to deliver. The internet and digital devices have provided solutions to the neverending demand for content and audience engagement. In theory, these are timesaving and have the potential to empower and enrich practice, as I described in Chapter Four. But the vastness of the world wide web requires great discipline to navigate without time-wasting. There are lessons to be learned in strategic usage.

Radio broadcasting is a vocation for many: a way of life that becomes an essential part of their identity and existence. For the practitioner addicted to the buzz of presenting and engaging with an audience, if removed from their station, they will have an urge to continue performing. Many independent local radio employees have been made redundant by the major commercial broadcasters, and consequently we are seeing a surge in launches of internet community stations and new podcasts. Some presenters have reached out to community stations to volunteer. My COVID-19 research findings revealed that community sector practitioners were imaginative and collaborative in their efforts to readjust when they were distanced from their stations. Assessed on their ability to deliver acceptable quality audio in sufficient quantity, they were motivated to adapt their domestic arrangements to studio-type activity and assemble the right equipment. As a minimum, a broadcast standard microphone and a laptop, or equivalent device, or smartphone sufficed. Some even experimented with building acoustic booths out of padded boxes or inside wardrobes.

Over time, station team members received extra training and under remote supervision adjusted to the new protocols, but my survey suggested that initially the better-equipped and skilled practitioners had to step in and work additional hours to cover their colleagues who found themselves unable to contribute as required. As these shifts in stations' practice-arrangements settle into a new normality, it raises the question of what a radio station can or should look like in the 21st century. There are certain established notions of what constitutes a radio station, and this set of physical infrastructural arrangements has fixed costs associated with it. If operators need to make savings in order to continue broadcasting, how might that impact on the buildings they use? Beyond the transmitter site and associated technical equipment, might the typical community radio station of the future become a dispersed arrangement of practitioners; a remodelled system based on free open source software (Correia et al., 2019)? Might more stations move into the homes of their team members, like at The Eye? At least Ofcom's stipulation that a studio must be located within the station's licensed area will avoid the worst case scenario of stations ending up like the internet station in Harpenden, with no physical or social hub to speak of.

The challenges associated with operating costs will only be exacerbated by the pandemic. Even though Ofcom brought forward their Community Radio Fund scheme to award money to community stations in the most desperate straits, allowed them all some leeway on the key commitments, and awarded additional short-term restricted service licences, it is doubtful that this support alone will be sufficient to keep the sector afloat longer term. There are other funding, lottery and charitable awards available, which stations can compete for, but revenue-generating schemes like selling media training and social skills services, running cafés and shops have fallen by the wayside. Stations relying on sales of airtime and sponsorship to local businesses have seen massive falls in income. It is understandable why there is lobbying for the government to do more. The third sector economy in the UK plays a pivotal role in providing support and services at the ground level, working with volunteers who invest their own time and effort, often at their own financial expense, to help others. This saves the country's institutions and the government a great deal of money and is aligned to the policy of giving local people more power over their own lives and neighbourhoods.[1] Community radio stations are uniquely positioned to raise public awareness of, and support these initiatives, *and* orchestrate their own projects which cater for the needs of their communities. These small, local media organizations contribute to social gain through their performances of localized public service broadcasting, which warrants a guaranteed subsidy framework for all of them.

Recommendations for future research and practice

During a research interview conducted in 2018, a station chairman told me: "The sector's incredibly challenged. I mean, you really wouldn't invent it, would you? Somebody did, but it's surprising it works!"

He was referring to the precarious nature of community radio, two years before the pandemic struck. He was right. If you were to prepare a business model working out how you could set up a station and staff it with the requisite technical experts, committed administrators and skilled practitioners, operating in a local marketplace, you would most likely give up. What fuels this sector is raw passion for the medium and the deep-seated desire to contribute to the greater good. Without teamwork, collaboration and cooperation, participation and engagement, none of it would be possible. Delivering a community radio service involves producing consistent volumes of local content, whether for broadcast or for posting online. It means building a community of practitioners with an enthusiasm for radio, music and entertainment as well as a shared connection to a geographical area comprising a range of places and people who reside and work there. Even social media requires a team effort if it is to be done efficiently to optimize visibility and engagement. Maintaining online presence effectively is a lot for one person to coordinate. Contributing to web pages, blogs, Twitter, Facebook and Instagram is ideally a collective endeavour, albeit one that needs overseeing to maintain standards and good behaviour.

Stations are autonomous and many are run democratically but there is a need for some sort of hierarchy so that members take responsibility for issues like health and safety, risk assessment, broadcasting standards, production and technical issues, and for working out solutions that are feasible and affordable, but also that reinforce and establish sustainable working environments and routines going forwards. Efficiency, time-keeping, comfort and security are no less a concern when work is being done on a voluntary basis and you are relying on the goodwill and availability of unrecompensed contributors. As the COVID-19 crisis unfolded, managers and governing boards across the sector were faced with unprecedented challenges, but in the vast majority of cases they were able to keep broadcasting because teamwork helped invigorate the symbiotic relationships with their listeners, target communities and other stakeholders. The situation brought into sharp relief the affordances of digital technologies and the capacity of practitioners across the sector to adapt and innovate.

As part of stations' community-oriented responses to the crisis, programmers provided additional content such as locally specific health and welfare updates alongside their usual information outputs. The lines of communication and personal connections that made such sourcing of content possible were already present, but the crisis prompted an escalation of interactional activity which could be sustained through online platforms. In a technologically connected world where everything seems to interweave, overlap and have a ripple effect, society has come to depend on certain devices and platforms for its socializing and for now, we are glad of it. As radio has evolved over time from sound broadcasting to multimedia communication, so community radio has earned its place alongside mainstream media in the sphere of cultural production: as a means of achieving media plurality reflecting under-represented groups in all their sociocultural, ethnic and geographically specific diversity.

Each station is different; there are similarities but there are divergences in each social site of practice-arrangements. This means that from a regulatory point of view, one size does not fit all. A flexible approach is required to regulate and support frameworks that can create a healthy environment for these individual organizations to grow and thrive. As the era of small-scale digital audio broadcasting (SSDAB) multiplexes dawns, it remains to be seen how the sector will evolve.

I urge community radio operators, in their enthusiasm to embrace new media's digital methods and platforms in pursuit of their pro-gramming and outreach goals, to not leave anyone behind. Harness technology without it dictating who can or cannot participate. The need to recruit volunteers and contributors from as wide a variety of social circles in the community as possible is tantamount. If commu-nity radio is true to its roots, it is about enabling everyone to freely, but respectfully, share their views, interests and perspectives on life. The internet and social media are not the panacea to all the practical, personal or physical limitations that may face those who would like, or indeed ought, to be included in the production activities of community radio broadcasting. There remain people in our neighbourhoods who do not yet possess the devices or the technical and media literacy skills that many of us take for granted: extra care should be taken to reach out to them, for that is the mantle bestowed upon the sector by the regulator. To achieve social gain objectives, we need to create fa-vourable environments for community to flourish both online and in the real world. Especially, in the real world. Whilst radio listening provides the companionship many of us yearn for, and social media and online platforms can enable interactivity and even simulate face-to-face encounters, I argue that it remains essential for a community radio station to have a physical hub: a place where tangible objects form part of the infrastructure of the operation, where the station is identifiably present, active and accessible *in* the locality.

Finally, I encourage researchers to conduct more rigorous studies into funding and staffing models in licensed community radio and independent online set-ups outside the mainstream, with a view to assessing and improving their chances for developing a sustainable way ahead. Findings may yield important insights into how financial viability can be attained whilst continuing to contribute to social gain: staying true to the underlying ideology, the raison d'être of the sector. The ethics of digital media are important to consider in this respect, but academics interested in mapping how technologies impact cultural production and media consumption, ought not overlook how their usage affects content producers. Innovations have changed how practitioners source, shape, share and store the content they produce, but not why they do it: the meaning the practice has in their lives. In the context of community radio, technologies have not altered what radio broadcasting means for communities of volunteers working as teams, striving in their spare time, or carving out the time in their busy lives, to put something back into the wider community which they call home. Radio is a technology, but it is used for communication and social interaction; it is about bringing people together in, and in relation to, the places where they co-exist.

Note

1 https://www.gov.uk/government/organisations/ministry-of-housing-communities-and-local-government (accessed 28.08.20.).

References

Bird, E.S., 2011. Are we all produsers now?. *Cult. Stud. 25* (4–5), pp. 502–516. 10.1080/09502386.2011.600532.

Bonini, T., *et al.*, 2014. Radio formats and social media use in Europe – 28 case studies of public service practice. *Radio. J. Int. Stud. Broadcast. Audio Media 12* (1–2), pp. 89–107. 10.1386/rjao.12.1-2.89_1.

Correia, R., Vieira, J., Aparicio, M., 2019. Community radio stations sustainability model: an open-source solution. *Radio. J. Int. Stud. Broadcast. Audio Media 17* (1), 29–45. 10.1386/rjao.17.1.29_1.

Speck, D., 2020. *Trust in Media.* European Broadcasting Union. Available from: https://www.ebu.ch/publications/research/login_only/report/trust-in-media (accessed 26.09.20.).

Zoellner, A., Lax, S., 2017. On-air and online: social media and local radio production in the UK. *Medien J. 39* (2), 5–18. 10.24989/medienjournal.v39i2.65.

Appendix

Table of community radio stations researched for this study

Fieldwork case studies	Geographical locations (by county/region)	Online questionnaire respondent stations (names are as submitted and anonymized where requested)
Internet radio station for Harpenden (unlicensed, defunct)	Hertfordshire	–
Vibe FM	Hertfordshire	–
103 The Eye	Leicestershire	–
Radio LaB	Bedfordshire	Radio LaB 97.1 FM
Radio Verulam	Hertfordshire	Radio Verulam
Somer Valley FM	Somerset	Somer Valley FM
	Dorset	Abbey 104
	Kent	Academy FM Folkestone
	Derbyshire	Amber Sound FM
	Hampshire	Andover Radio
	Lancashire	Beyond Radio
	Cambridgeshire	Black Cat Radio
	West Midlands	Black Country Radio
	Argyll and Bute (Scotland)	Bute Island Radio
	Cambridgeshire	Cambridge 105 Radio
	Essex	Chelmsford Community Radio
	Bedfordshire	Diverse FM
	Argyll and Bute (Scotland)	Dunoon Community Radio (DCR 97.4 FM)
	Cumbria	Eden FM
	Derbyshire	Erewash Sound
	Surrey	Kane FM 103.7

Fieldwork case studies	*Geographical locations (by county/region)*	*Online questionnaire respondent stations (names are as submitted and anonymized where requested)*
	Moray (Scotland)	Keith Community Radio
	Berkshire	Kennet Radio
	Leicestershire	Kohinoor Radio
	Northumberland	Lionheart Radio
	Northamptonshire	NLive Radio
	West London	Nomad Radio
	Norfolk	Park Radio
	Dorset	Purbeck Coast FM
	Tyne and Wear	Radio Tyneside
	Buckinghamshire	Red Kite Radio
	Somerset	Sedgemoor FM
	Lincolnshire	Siren Radio
	North and West Yorkshire	Tempo 107.4 FM
	Cheshire	The Cat Community Radio
	Isle of Wight	Vectis Radio
	Buckinghamshire	Wycombe Sound
	South East England	*4 × anon*
	South West England	*3 × anon*
	West Midlands	*anon*
	Northern Ireland	*anon*
	Scotland	*anon*

Index

About Harpenden 45
Access Radio 28
advertising 29
Ahva, Laura 30
Aldridge, Meryl 11
alternative media 21
AM waveband 28–9
AMARC. *see* Association Mondiale
  Des Radiodiffuseurs
  Communautaires
archiving systems 87
Argentina 21
Arnheim, Rudolf 4
Art of radio, The 6
Association Mondiale Des
  Radiodiffuseurs
  Communautaires 20
Atton, Chris 10
Audacity 88
audience: as community 11; of
  community radio 9–12; surveying
  of 89
audio editing 88
Audition 59
Australia 20
automated playout systems 111

BBC: bimedia reporting requirements
  81; content control by 23;
  establishment of 23; local stations
  24; listening groups used by 106;
  Local Democracy Reporting
  service 84; Memorandum of
  Understanding with 56, 84; music-
  based Light programme of 24; as
  national system 23; programme
  restructuring by 24; Radio 2, 24
BBC Radio 1, 24
Berry, Richard 6
Bird, Elizabeth 8, 107
BJTC. *see* Broadcast Journalism
  Training Council
Blackburn, Tony 24, 110
Bonini, Tiziano 7, 19
Brand, Graham 5
Brecht, Berthold 4, 6
British Broadcasting Company.
  see BBC
British community radio: description
  of 22; licensing of 22–3; regulation
  of 22–5
Brittan, Leon 27
Broadcast Journalism Training
  Council 59
Broadcasting Act of 1990 25
Bruns, Axel 8–9
Buckley, Steve 27
Bush Radio 29

campus-based community
  radio 58–61
Canada 20
Canstream 29, 59, 80
Centre for Contemporary Cultural
  Studies 24
Chelmsford Community Radio 97
Chiltern Radio 28
citizen journalism 83, 107

CMA. *see* Community Media
Association
Colombia 21
COMCOM. *see* Community
Communications Group
"coming up later announcements," 66
Communications Act 28
Communications Radio Order 28
Community Broadcasting
Association of Australia 20
Community Communications
Group 27
community media: global dimensions
of 10; multiplicity of 21; social
engagement by 21
Community Media Association 29,
36, 56, 80
community radio: audiences of 9–12;
business of 109–12; campus-based
58–61; digital technologies' effect
on 9; diversity in 89–93; as field of
study 10; funding of 114; future
research for 112–5; global
development of 19; home-
produced local content 44–9; as
"in-betweeners," 30, 85; licence for
83; local content provided by 31,
113–4; national regulatory
frameworks for 20; nature of 19;
not-for-profit organizations 30;
online spaces of 79–80; periods of
17; principles of 114; purpose of 19;
staffing of 114; sustainability of
115; United Nations support for 19
Community Radio Association 20,
27, 29
Community Radio Fund 36
Community Radio Fund Panel 100
community radio stations: automated
playout systems used by 111;
autonomous nature of 113;
business of 109–10; content
creation by 111; differences among
32–3; ethnic and racial diversity at
92; global growth of 21; list of
116–7; physical location of 114;
practice-centric approach to 34;
public awareness by 112;
researching of 32–5; social media
use by 110; staffing of 110;

sustainability of 110–1;
see also radio stations
conferences 18
Couldry, Nick 10
COVID-19 2, 18, 22, 33, 38–40, 57,
61, 67, 73–4, 76–7, 79, 93–100,
104, 113
CRA. *see* Community Radio
Association
"creative amateurism" 24
Crook, Tim 6

Dagron, Alfonso Gumucio 21
Days of Our Lives 64
De Vuyst, Sara 90
Denmark 20
digital technologies: community
radio affected by 9, 108;
democratic participation uses of 8;
description of 2, 6–9; embracing of
114; ethics of 115; international
engagement increased through 18;
local coverage affected by 83–4,
109; practitioners' use of 108; radio
content produced using 81–9; radio
station operations maintained by,
during COVID-19 77; radio studies
affected by 35
digitization 105
disc jockeys 24
"dispersed" activities 38
Disruptions 90
diversity 89–93
*Diversity and equal opportunities in
radio* 92

EAR. *see* ethnographic action
research
Eckersley, Peter 23
ECREA. *see* European
Communication Research and
Education Association
electronic agora 19
Environment Matters 64
ethnographic action research 20
European Communication
Research and Education
Association 9, 17
Everett, Kenny 24

Facebook 7, 18, 51, 57, 80, 106
films 4
Finland 20
FM waveband 28–9
For the People 28
Forms of talk 5
France 19
FTP. *see* For the People

Giddens, Anthony 5
Gillard, Frank 24
"global village," 4
Goffman, Erving 5
Gordon, Janey 58
Guattari, Felix 19

Harpenden 78, 80, 112
Hendy, David 8
Herts Advertiser 70–1
Hilmes, Michele 7
HOH Show 58
How to do community radio 19
Howley, Kevin 10
hyperlocal journalism 31

IAMCR. *see* International
　Association for Media and
　Communications Research
IBA. *see* Independent Broadcasting
　Authority
Ibrahim, Zane 29
ICA. *see* International
　Communication Association
ILR. *see* independent local radio
　stations
"in-betweeners," 30, 85
Independent Broadcasting Authority
　25, 28
independent local radio stations
　24, 28
Independent Radio News 51, 63
information technology 1
Instagram 18
International Association for Media
　and Communications Research 18
International Communication
　Association 17
International Radio Journalism, 6
internet: online inquiries 38–9; online

spaces 79–80; opportunities offered
　by 7; *see also* websites
internet stations 26
Invisible medium, The 27
Ireland 25
IRN. *see* Independent Radio News
Italy 19

Jankowski, Nicholas 21–2
Journal of Radio & Audio Media 6

Keith Community Radio 96, 99
Kennet Radio 95
King, Gretchen 17, 19

Lacey, Kate 8
League of Nations' International
　Committee on Intellectual
　Cooperation 19
Leicester 24
live shows 68–70
Live Wire, 50
LLR Media 90
local content: community radio
　provision of 31, 113–4; COVID-19
　effects on production of 93–100;
　description of 31–2; digital
　technologies for coverage of 83–4,
　109; presenters for 84; Radio
　Verulam 92.6 FM coverage of
　63–5; UK community radio
　coverage of 31, 107–8
Local Life programme 64
Local Radio Alliance 90
local radio stations: branding of 78;
　community building at 49–74;
　content production at 49–74;
　COVID-19 effects on local content
　production at 93–100; crisis response
　by 101; crisis-management decisions
　at 94; enduring value of 107–9;
　funding of 77–8; income sources for
　56; listenership of 80; 103 The Eye
　49–52, 78, 116; physical environment
　of 76; programme schedules at 96–8;
　public service role of 98; Radio LaB
　97.1 FM 49, 58–61, 79–80, 91, 95–6,
　116; Radio Verulam 92.6 FM.
　see Radio Verulam 92.6 FM;

researching of 32–5; Somer
Valley 97.5 FM 49, 55–8, 84,
92, 99, 116; timing on 51–2;
traffic reports on 54; Vibe 107.6 FM
49, 52–5, 79, 110, 116; volunteers
at 108–9; weather reports on 54;
websites of 55, 57; "what's
ons," 50–1; *see also* radio
stations
locality 11
Long, Janice 110
Luci Live 86
Luton Buzz 59

MacBride, Sean 19
MacBride Report 19
*Making waves: stories of participatory
communication for social
change* 20–1
Many Voices, One World 19
Marconi, Guglielmo 4
Marconi company 23
Marine Broadcasting Offences Act 24
Massey, Doreen 11
McLuhan, Marshall 4
McWhinnie, Donald 6
MeCCSA. *see* Media,
Communication and Cultural
Studies Association
Media, Communication and Cultural
Studies Association 18
media consumers 8
media technology: community-
connectedness of 11; shifts in 8;
see also digital technologies
Melton, Mowbray 50
Memorandum of Understanding
with BBC 56, 84
"microbroadcasters," 8
Microsoft Onedrive 59
Moores, Shaun 5
Moylan, Katie 76
"Myth of community studies,
The," 10

news: as local service 11–2, 24–5,
31–3, 108; gathering of 50, 56, 59,
63–6; standards 83–5; under
lockdown 99–101

New World Information and
Communication Order 19
"newszak" 85
NGO. *see* non-governmental
organizations
Nguyen, An 85
non-governmental organizations 20
Norway 20
not-for-profit organizations 30

OB. *see* outside broadcast
Ofcom 25–6, 32, 44, 55, 61, 77, 84,
89–90, 92–3, 100
103 The Eye 49–52, 78, 116
online inquiry 38–9
Ontario Association of Campus
Broadcasters 20
ontological security 5
outside broadcast 12, 53, 70–2
Outspoken 64

PAR. *see* participatory action
research
Parents Show, The 68
participant observation 37–8
participatory action research 20
participatory communication 20–1
piracy 25–6
podcasting: as audio output
55, 61, 69, 89, 106, 111;
platforms for 64, 80; practice of
6–7, 101, 105
Possibilities for local radio 24
Powell, Rachel 24
practice-as-research 2, 33, 37,
practice theory 34–5
*Practice turn in contemporary theory,
The* 34
pre-recorded content 65–7
produsage 9
"produser," 8
"profanity button," 53
propaganda 4
Public Broadcasting Association of
Australia 20
public service broadcasting 31

radio: advanced theorization of 5;
change in 105–7; communication

purposes of 115; democratizing power of 106; meaning of 6–9; personality of 54; programme schedules used in 105–6; progress in 105–7; propaganda uses of 4; public trust in 107; as screen medium 7; social aspects of 9; as social medium 4–6; *see also* community radio
Radio: critical concepts in media and cultural studies 6
radio audiences 9–12
radio broadcasting: discursive characteristics of 12; global context of 17–22; history of 4; intangible aspect of 108; multimedia 106; phenomenological aspects of 5; sociable characteristics of 12; UK regulations on 23; as way of life 111
Radio Caroline 24
Radio content in the digital age 9
Radio Days Africa 18
Radio Free Europe 17
Radio Journal, The 6
Radio LaB 97.1 FM 49, 58–61, 79–80, 91, 95–6, 116
Radio Liberty 17
radio listening: benefits of 12; as daily ritual 6; evolution of 8
Radio Luxembourg 24
radio medium: affective immateriality of 4; research on 5
radio production: digital technologies in 81–9; studying of 35–6
radio programming: online sources used in 85–6; social media in 7
Radio Regen 90
radio stations: as community place 77–9; crisis response by 101; multimedia content created by 8; multimedia output from 106; off-air activities for promoting 106–7; physical environment of 76, 111–2; researching of 36; shaping of content 88; sharing of output 88; storing of information 87–8; surveying of audience by 89; *see also* local radio stations; *see also* community radio stations

radio studies: advancements in 6; resurgence of 17
Radio Studies Network, The 6
Radio Sutatenza 21
Radio Takeover Show 61
Radio Today 90
Radio Tyneside 96
Radio Verulam 92.6 FM 116; at-home broadcasting 73; branding of 78; "coming up later announcements" on 66; commitments of 63; description of 62–3; director-level members at 72; diversity at 92; hierarchical structure of 79; live shows on 68–70; local current affairs coverage by 63–5; lockdown response at 73–4; outside broadcasts 70–2; pre-recorded content on 65–7; programme schedules at 97; reporting 70–2; Sky News use by 63; studio bookings on 65; teamwork 72–3; training 72–3; voice-tracking on 67–8; website of 64
radiocracy 6
Raw Vibes 55
Razer Seiren microphone 59
Remarkable Harpenden 37, 46, 48
restricted service licences 27, 58
Rockefeller Foundation 20
RSLs. *see* restricted service licences

St Albans 62, 70–1
Scannell, Paddy 5
Schatzki, Theodore 35, 38
Second World War 4
self-discipline 86
Sieveking, Lance 4
Sixties Vinyl Countdown 50
Sky News 63
small-scale digital audio broadcasting 26, 90, 114
smartphone: apps 86; radio production uses of 46–7, 60, 69–71, 87, 111; researchers' use of 34
snapshot visits 37–8
"Snoop," 72
social activism 19–20

social engagement 21
social media: building of 18; community radio stations' use of 110; interactivity benefits of 114; presenter promotion using 66; Radio LaB 59, 80; in radio programming 7
"social site" 35, 76, 82, 114
"social sonic space," 11
soft journalism 77
Somer Valley 97.5 FM 49, 55–8, 84, 92, 99, 116
Somer Valley Education Trust, The 56
Sound Broadcasting Act, The 24
SSDAB. *see* small-scale digital audio broadcasting
Stacey, Margaret 10
Stafford's World 50
Sweden 20
syndicated shows 45, 50

tabloidization 85
Tacchi, Jo 6
"Talk, identity and performance," 5
Talk of the Town 33
Talking Newspaper 73, 98
Team Viewer 60
Telecommunications Act 25
television programmes 4
text messaging 7
#TheNewNormal 18
Theorising media and practice 34
traffic reports 54
Twitter 7, 18, 51, 57, 80

UK community radio: in COVID-19 pandemic 100; demand for 23–4; funding of 29–31; history of 20; independent local radio stations 28; licensing of 22–3, 27–9; local content provided by 31; non-mainstream 22–32; overview of 16–7; piracy in 25–6; regulation of 22–5; restricted service licences for 27; sustaining of 29–31; undervaluing of 22; websites of 79
UK Community Radio Network 38, 90
UKCRN. *see* UK Community Radio Network
Understanding alternative media, 21
Understanding media: the extensions of man, 4
UNESCO. *see* United Nations Educational, Scientific and Cultural Organization
United Nations Educational, Scientific and Cultural Organization 18–19

Verulam Sport 69
Vibe 107.6 FM 49, 52–5, 79, 110, 116
voice-tracking 54, 61, 67–8, 95–96

Watford Observer, The 54
weather reports 54
Web 2.0 interconnectivity 8
websites: of community radio stations 79–80; description of 7; editing of material for 88; Radio Verulam 92.6 FM 64; sifting through 86
"what's ons," 50–1
Wireless Telegraphy Act of 1949 24
World Association of Community Radio Broadcasters 20

Zoom Corporation 46